Acoustic Solo Series

Acoustic Blues Solos

Project Manager: Aaron Stang
Cover Design: Todd Ellison
Layout: Candy Woolley
Production Coordinator: Karl Bork

© 2005 WARNER BROS. PUBLICATIONS

Any duplication, adaptation or arrangement of the compositions
contained in this collection requires the written consent of the Publisher.
No part of this book may be photocopied or reproduced in any
way without permission. Unauthorized uses are an infringement
of the U.S. Copyright Act and are punishable by law.

ABOUT THE ARTISTS

MIKE DOWLING
Influenced by traditional Piedmont-style finger pickers like Mississippi John Hurt and swing jazz legends like the late George Barnes, Mike has developed a style uniquely his own. Early in his career, Mike toured and recorded with mandolinist Jethro Burns, jazz violin great Joe Venuti, and master fiddler Vassar Clements. Clements calls him simply "One of the finest guitar players there is, anywhere." In 1995, after years of playing with various ensembles, Mike launched a solo career. With the release of his first solo album, the critically acclaimed *Swamp Dog Blues,* he began headlining at concerts and festivals throughout the world and has been a frequent guest on public radio's "A Prairie Home Companion." Mike maintains a busy performance schedule and teaches at a variety of music camps and workshops throughout the country, including his own Greater Yellowstone Music Camp for acoustic blues and swing.

AL PETTEWAY
Al Petteway has had an illustrious career as a guitarist, composer, and producer. He has been featured on more than 60 nationally released recordings, including 14 of his own. His original compositions have been used in movie soundtracks and for programs on NPR and PBS, including Ken Burns' film *Mark Twain.* His trademark musical style, mixing Celtic and American themes, has won him more than 50 Music Association awards, including the Indie award for *Gratitude,* a duo guitar project with his wife and musical partner, Amy White. Al is the coordinator for the world-renowned Swannanoa Gathering's Guitar Week and is Artist-in-Residence at Warren Wilson College near Asheville, North Carolina. When they aren't touring as a duo, he and Amy work together, recording music and photographing nature at their home high in the mountains of western North Carolina.

KENNY SULTAN
Kenny Sultan is one of the most highly respected blues guitarists, and blues guitar educators, in the country. Kenny graduated with honors from the University of California at Santa Barbara, where he majored in music/ethnomusicology. A noted teacher, he has taught music, guitar, and music history at the university level and has conducted countless workshops and seminars. In addition to numerous recordings as a sideman, Kenny has two widely acclaimed solo guitar CDs with Solid Air Records.

CONTENTS

Title	Artist	Page	CD Track
Bottleneck March	Mike Dowling	6	1
Cascade Rag	Kenny Sultan	12	2
If the Shoe Fits	Kenny Sultan	19	3
Eureka Hotel	Al Petteway	24	4
Fishin' in the Wind	Mike Dowling	30	5
Honky Tonk	Kenny Sultan	36	6
Johnson City Rag	Mike Dowling	42	7
Lightnin' Strikes	Kenny Sultan	49	8
Meant to Be	Al Petteway	56	9
Minor Thing	Mike Dowling	61	10
Rosalie	Mike Dowling	70	11
The Sick Boogie	Kenny Sultan	76	12
Standard Tuning Track			13
Open D Tuning Track			14
Open G Tuning Track			15
DADGAD Tuning Track			16

PERFORMANCE NOTES

BOTTLENECK MARCH - Mike Dowling

This tune was written as a result of exploring the idea of combining high-register melody notes, either fretted or bottlenecked, with open low-register bass notes. That kind of musical spread has always appealed to me. You'll find a variety of fingerpicking techniques in this piece, from forward rolls in the intro to the quirky syncopations of what my wife calls the "cartoon" ending. Some melody notes in the main theme that sound like a "pinch" (thumb and fingers playing simultaneously) are generated by slides and pull-offs. Practice these passages slowly in order to build up speed for a less frantic sound when you kick the tempo up. Although the theme repeats itself, I've transcribed the slight variations in each repetition just as I recorded them.

CASCADE RAG - Kenny Sultan

"Cascade Rag" is a ragtime blues piece. It starts off on the B part, or bridge, which is a little unusual, but then it evolves into the typical V-I-V-I-V-I turnaround pattern. I use several different positions for the chords to keep it interesting. Once you master it, try to add a few of them yourself. There are a few tricky right-hand rolls, so be sure to start slowly and then work it up to speed. Good luck!

IF THE SHOE FITS - Kenny Sultan

"If the Shoe Fits" has a bit of a jazzy feel to it because of the slides and 9th chords. I make partial 9ths instead of complete 9ths in this song, which helps smooth out the slides. Before you start the slide, be sure to get a nice big sound going to help carry the tone throughout the measure.

EUREKA HOTEL - Al Petteway

Here's a great use for DADGAD tuning: Play the melody in parallel octaves on three pairs of strings. The repeating bass notes on the downbeat keep this tune rolling along, and the melody comes right out of the chords. Many times, my fingers are holding down the entire chord even when I play only one or two notes of it. That way, I'm safe if I hit one of the other strings by accident or if I want to fill out the chord a bit more.

FISHIN' IN THE WIND - Mike Dowling

This is my solo version of what was originally a guitar duet I wrote for my "Two of a Kind" CD, recorded with Pat Donohue. This tune is played in a hybrid picking style, using a combination of both fingerpicking and plectrum playing. To do this, you hold the flatpick like usual while using your middle and ring fingers to get a fingerpicked, alternating bass sound. The reason for incorporating the pick in this tune is to give a little extra crispness to the bass runs and the other picked passages. I would consider the syncopations in this piece to be of medium difficulty. The hardest thing about playing it will be getting used to holding the pick while using your fingers. Try to work through it slowly and you'll be rewarded in the end with a new technique to add to your bag.

HONKY TONK - Kenny Sultan

This song also deviates a little from my tendencies in that it is a 12-bar blues in the key of C. The hardest parts for me are the numerous runs and double-bassing (two bass notes per beat). There is definitely a Big Bill Broonzy thing going on here. Play this song slowly and with feeling, just as you would a standard blues.

JOHNSON CITY RAG - Mike Dowling

I first performed this ragtime tune in Johnson City, Tennessee. It's in the key of A and has several parts, each affording accompaniment by low-register bass notes. On the recording I'm playing with a thumbpick and bare fingers. I like the idea of digging in with my thumb and muting the bass strings for a little more aggressive sound, as opposed to the ringing bass that often gives ragtime guitar pieces an element of staid propriety. But maybe that's just me. In order to articulate the high E7 passage, I've used pull-offs while playing an alternating bass. Be patient as you work on this. Build up speed slowly and I think you'll find the tune will come together smoothly.

LIGHTNIN' STRIKES - Kenny Sultan

This is a typical call-and-response kind of blues in the key of E. I bounce between rhythm and lead or fills. I use a lot of double-stops (two notes at once) to give it some extra kick. Also, by resting your right hand on the bass strings, you create a more percussive quality by muting the low E and A string a bit. Check out the CD to hear what I'm talking about.

MEANT TO BE - Al Petteway

In DADGAD, the key of Am lends itself nicely to blues styles. On this tune I set up a rhythmic pattern with my right hand hitting the strings on beats 2 and 4, rather than on every beat. This creates a nice backbeat to play the melody over. The same technique is used as in "Alphonso Brown," where any notes that fall on 2 or 4 must be played with the back of the nails to maintain the rhythmic pattern. Many times I'll stretch notes up without releasing them or start notes at the top of a stretch and bring them down. Both of these techniques sound great on acoustic guitar.

MINOR THING - Mike Dowling

I recorded this song, which I wrote with a fiddle-playing friend of mine, twice. The version transcribed here is for solo fingerstyle guitar as I play it on my "String Crazy" CD. After first having performed the song in ensemble format using a pick, I wanted to approach it differently as a solo piece. When playing the eighth-note passages, I usually use a thumb stroke for a note on the beat and a finger-plucked note for the "ands;" but upon closer listening when I was transcribing this tune, I realized that in the second half of my solo version I gravitate to something altogether different as far as the picking is concerned. In the second half I'm holding my thumb and forefinger together as if I were holding a flatpick. This technique accounts for the different tone you'll hear on my downstrokes, where there's almost a "click" to be heard along with the note.

ROSALIE - Mike Dowling

This is my arrangement for solo guitar of a Civil War era song, "Rosalie, the Prairie Flower", written by George Root. Root wrote other familiar songs of the era, among them "The Battle Cry of Freedom" and "Tramp, Tramp, the Boys Are Marching." I learned the basic melody from a friend of mine who, in turn, had learned it from old piano sheet music he had come across. I arranged "Rosalie" for G tuning and in the process I slowed it down drastically from what my buddy had played for me; so much so that I felt it needed a little rhythmic resuscitation to keep the song from becoming musically amorphous. I began experimenting with a backbeat and stumbled upon a technique that worked for me. You'll notice I use a similar brush-type backbeat in "Rocky Road." I also wrote an introduction for "Rosalie" that shows up later in the tune as an interlude using a C minor 6 chord; another somewhat stark departure from mid-1800's pop music. As a composer I find myself getting as much satisfaction from arranging someone else's music as I do from creating my own, and after years of doing this I find myself gravitating more toward slower compositions which offer more possibilities for self-expression. For me, at least, it's easier to paint my initials on a slow-moving boxcar than it is on an express train.

THE SICK BOOGIE - Kenny Sultan

"The Sick Boogie" is just that: a boogie in the key of A that got out of control. We were messing around in the studio, playing fast and proud, and they happened to be running tape. I use fingerstyle technique here, but it could almost be done with a flatpick. It is basically similar in nature to our other blues—but hyper-speed. I alternate between my right-hand thumb and index finger for the lead parts. This song is way more feel than technique, so let it fly!

Bottleneck March

By MIKE DOWLING

Open D tuning *(w/slide)*:

⑥ = D   ③ = F#
⑤ = A   ② = A
④ = D   ① = D

Moderately fast

*w/slide.

**Up-stem notes played w/slide.

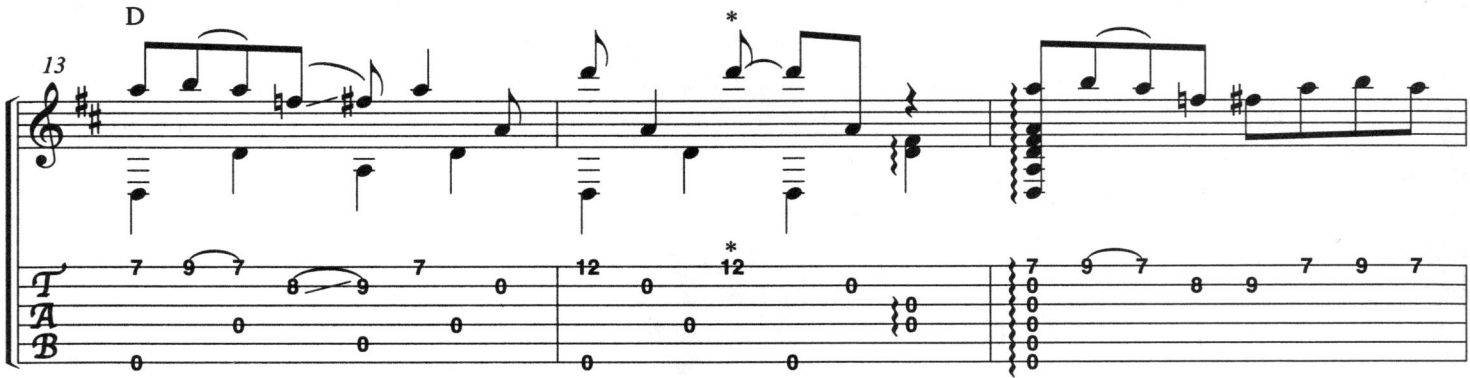

Bottleneck March - 6 - 1
SAIR011

© 1991 TableTop Music (ASCAP) and Solid Air Music (ASCAP)
All Rights Reserved

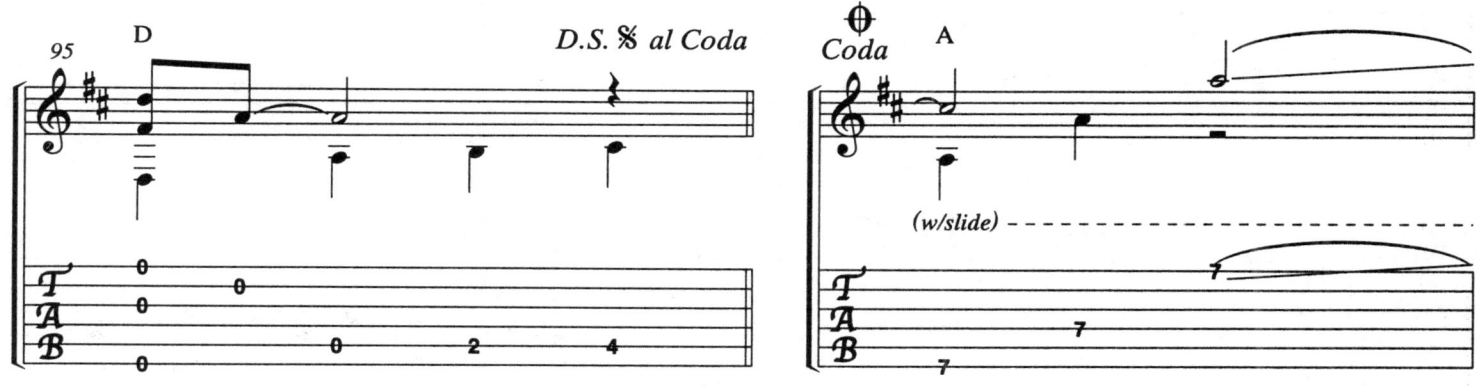
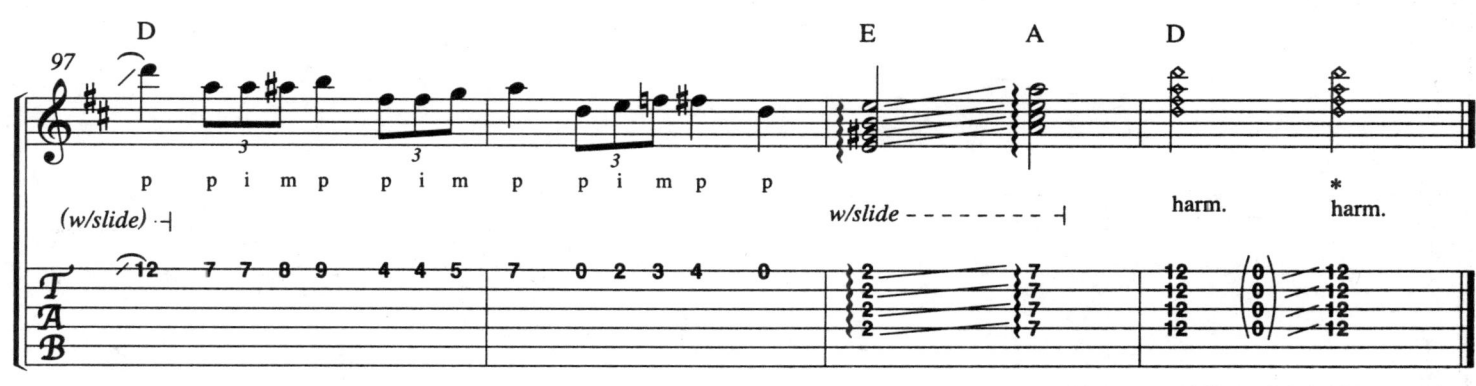

*Place slide between nut & first fret with harmonic still ringing & slide up to 12th fret.

Cascade Rag

By KENNY SULTAN

Moderately fast ragtime, in 2 ♩ = 120

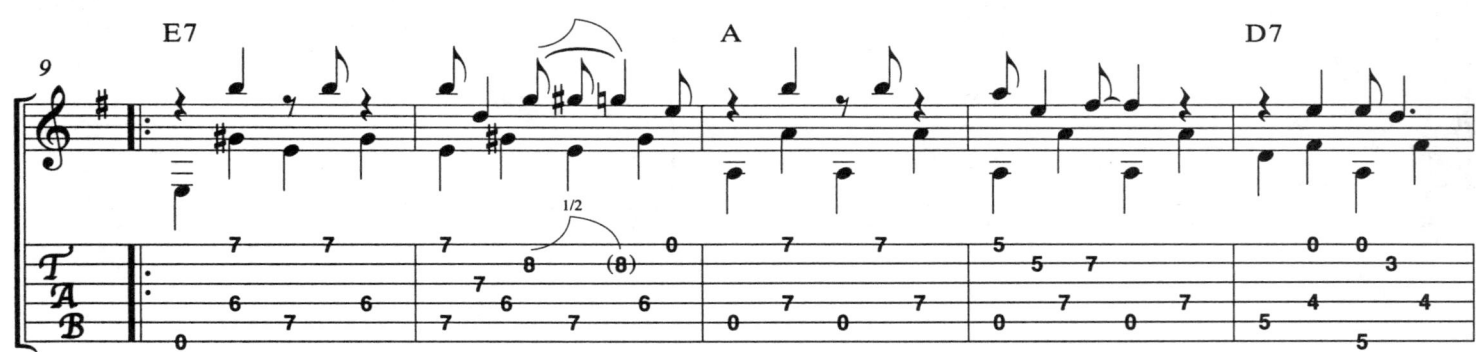

Cascade Rag - 7 - 1
SAIR011

© 2002 Original Solid Air Records Music (BMI)
All Rights Reserved

13

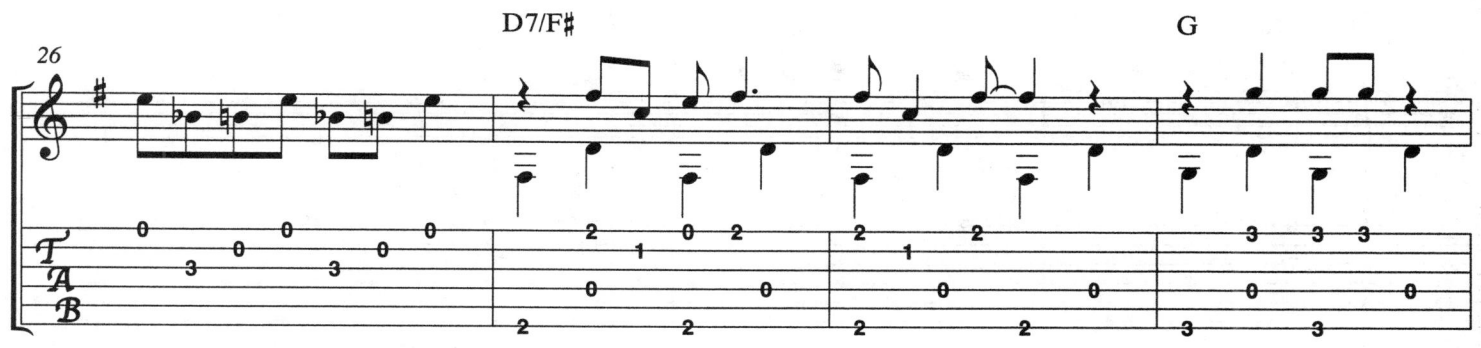

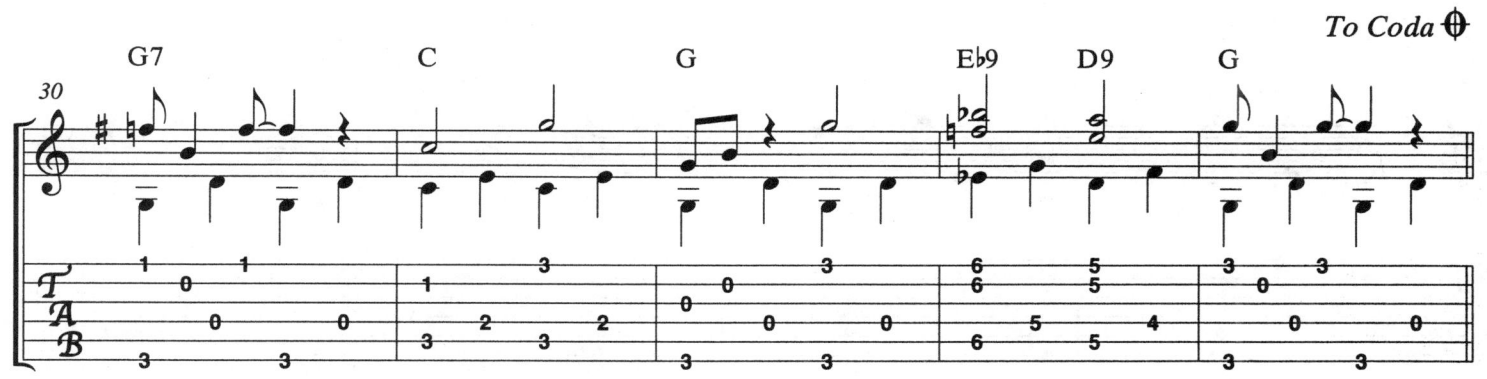

14

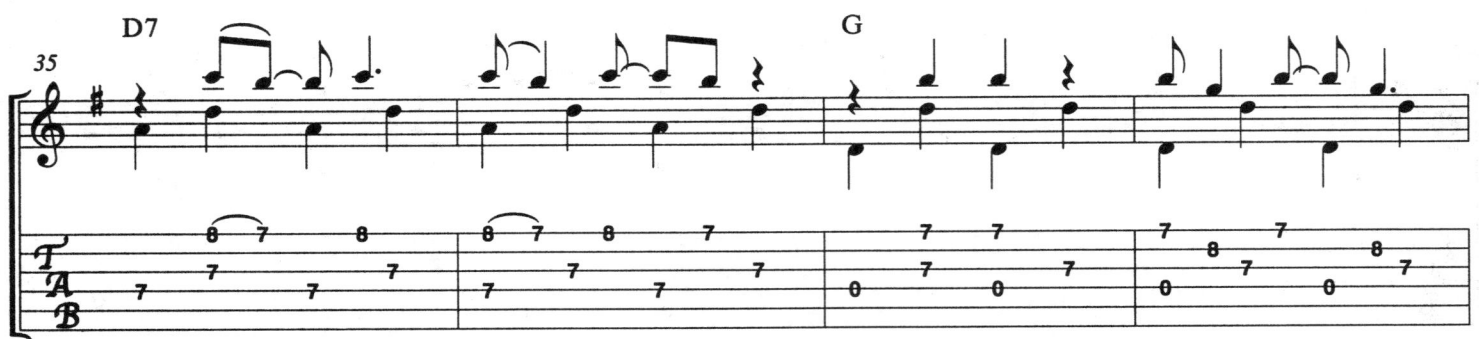

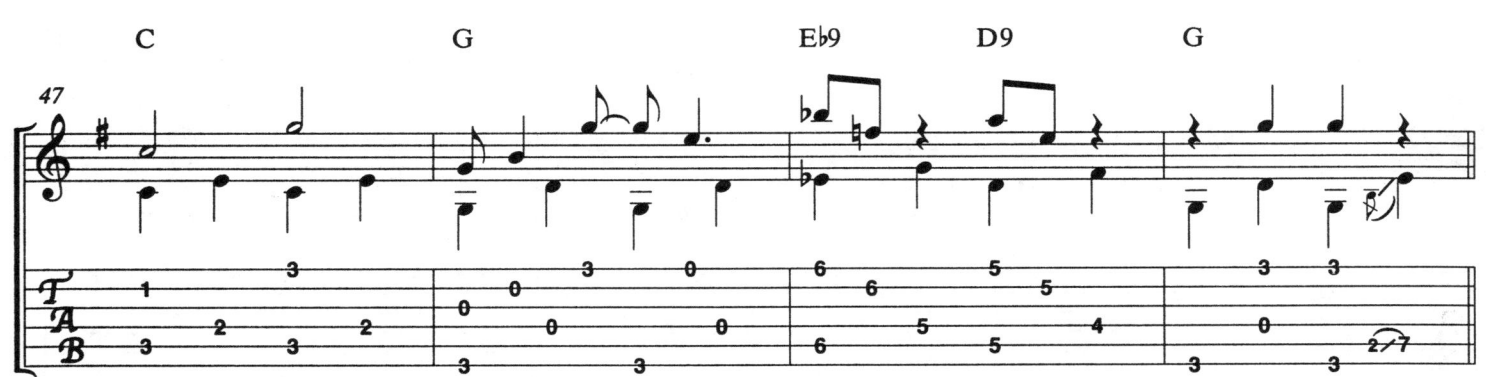

Cascade Rag - 7 - 3
SAIR011

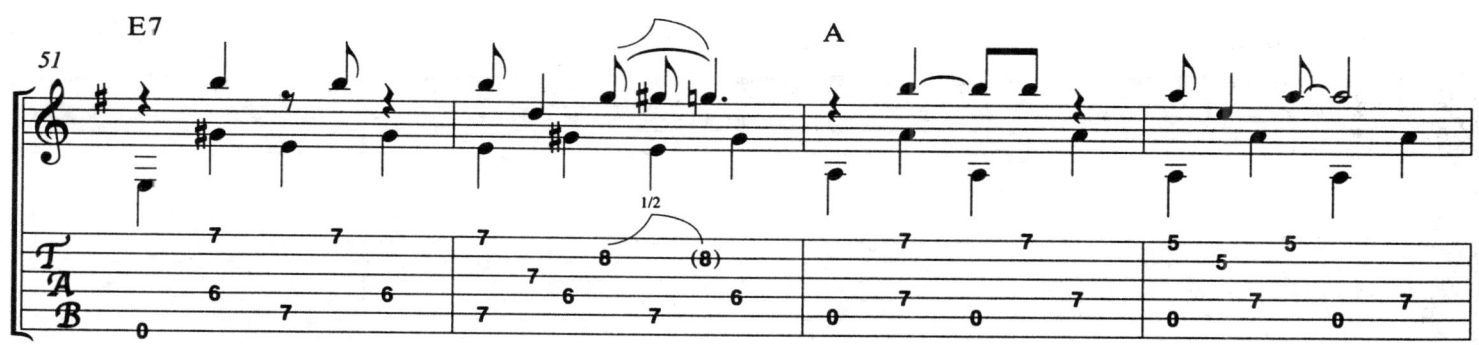
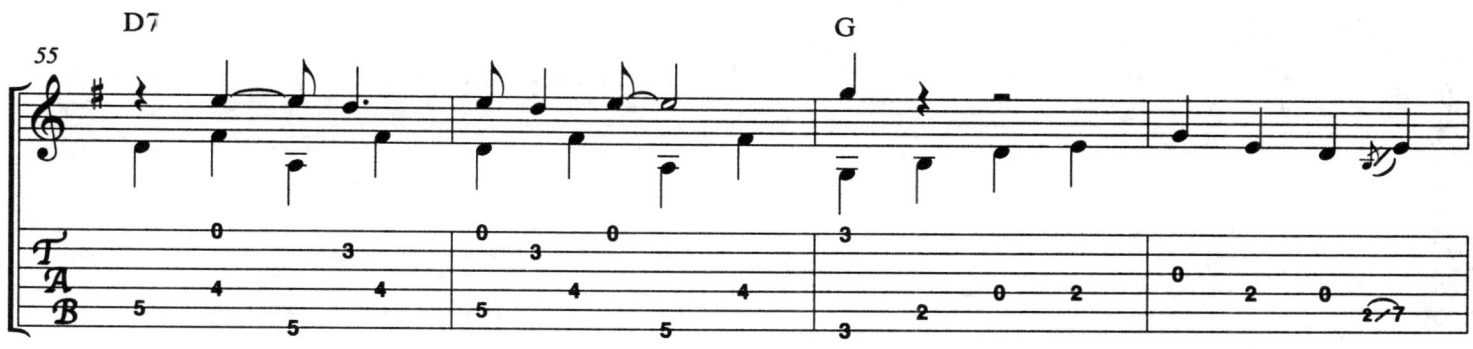
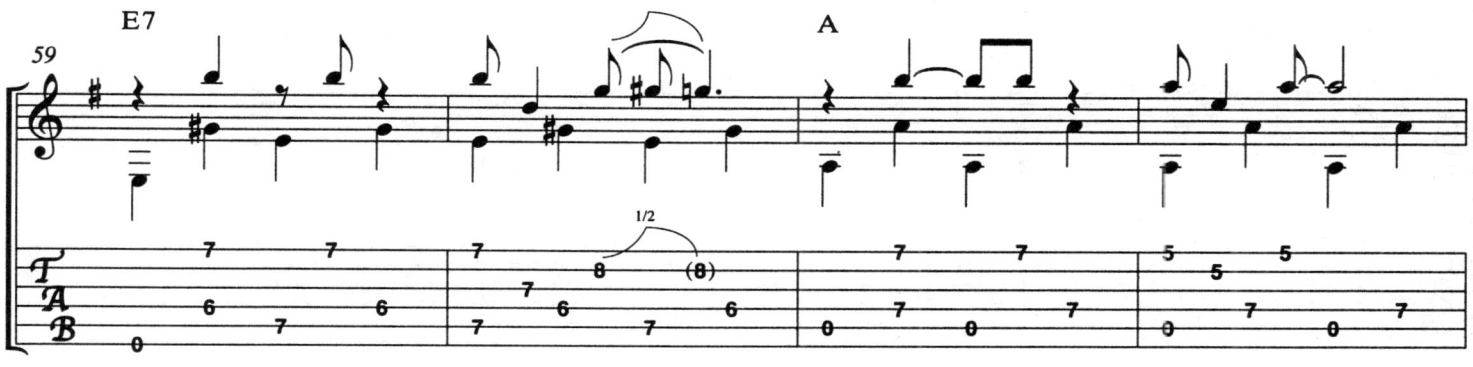
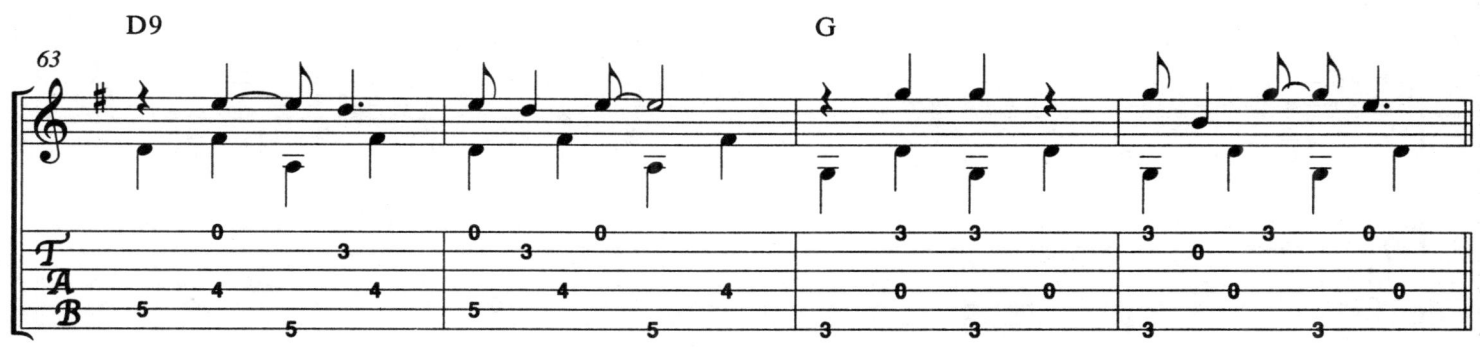

16

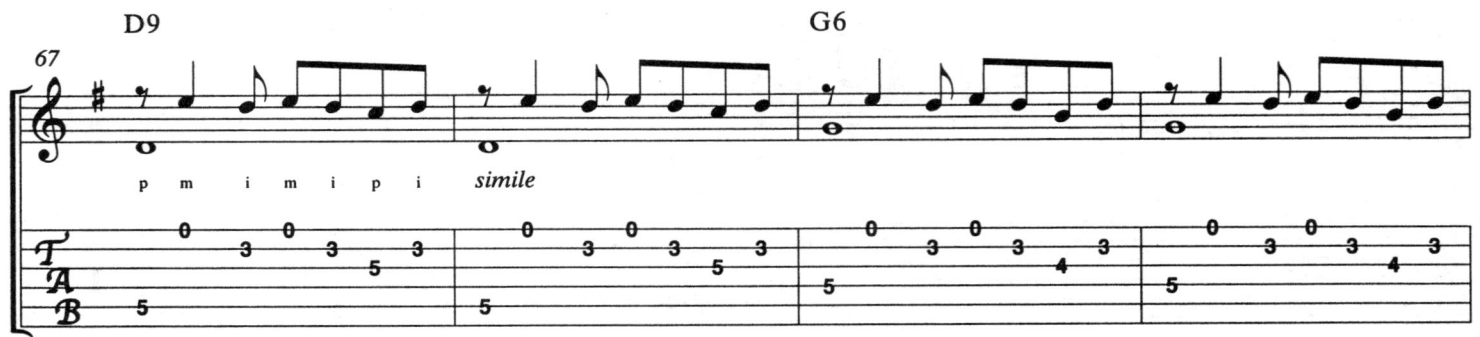

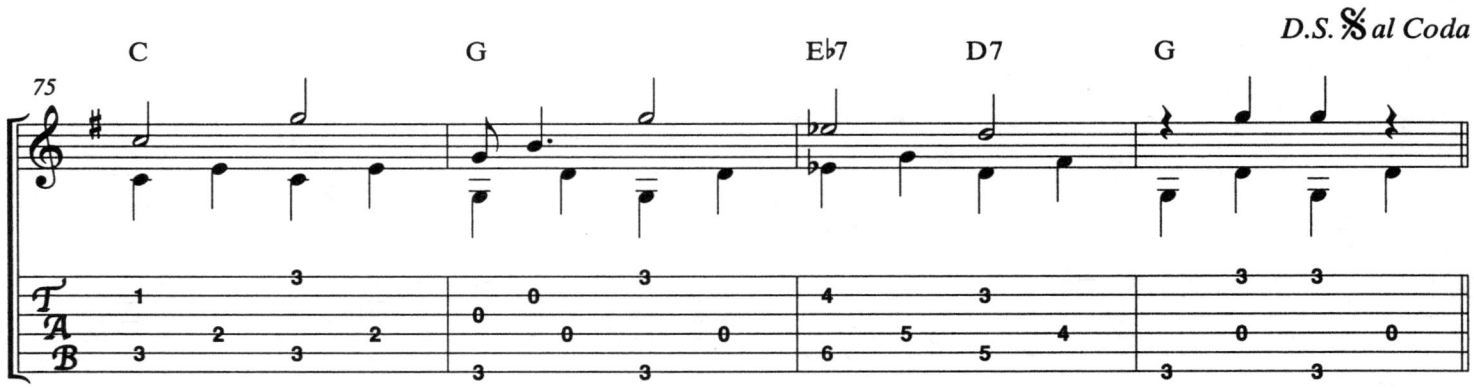

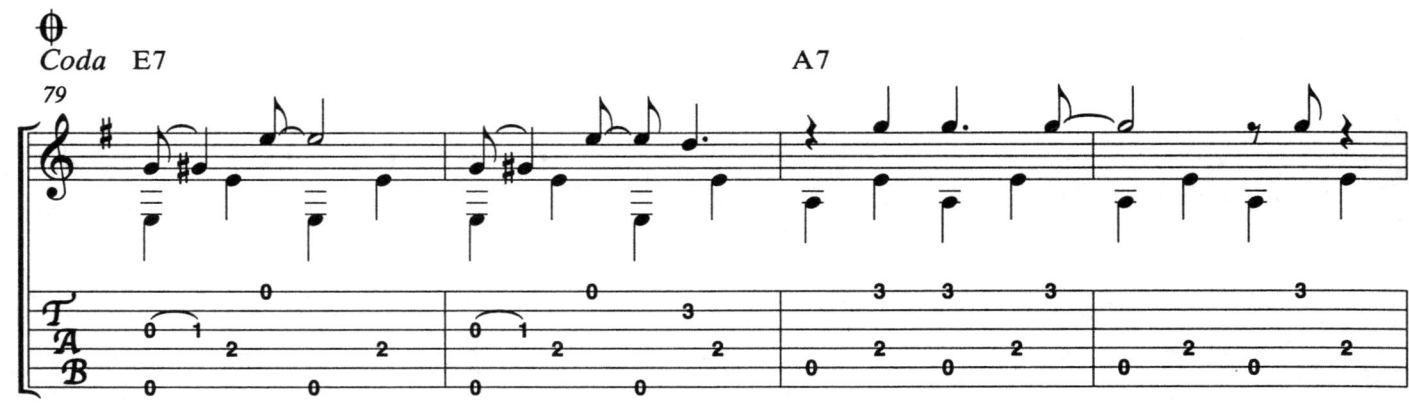

17

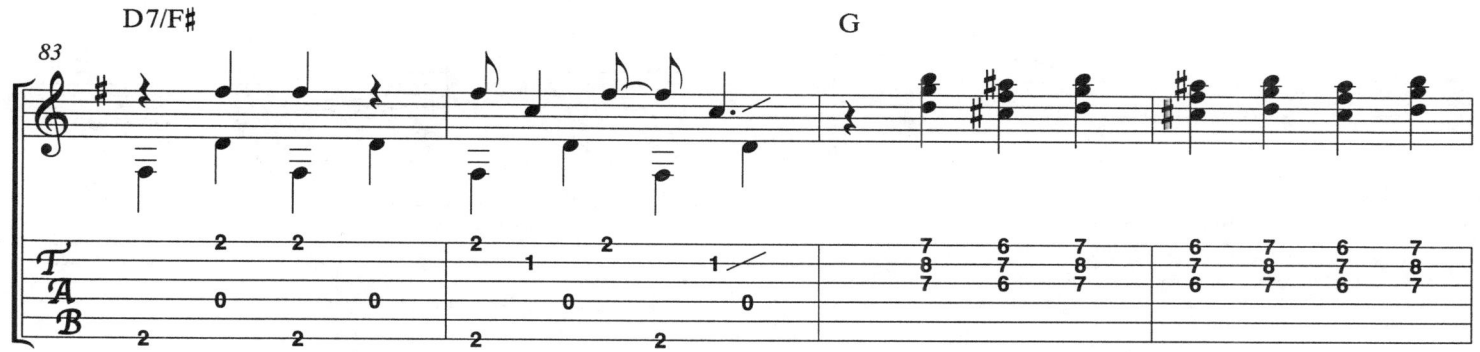
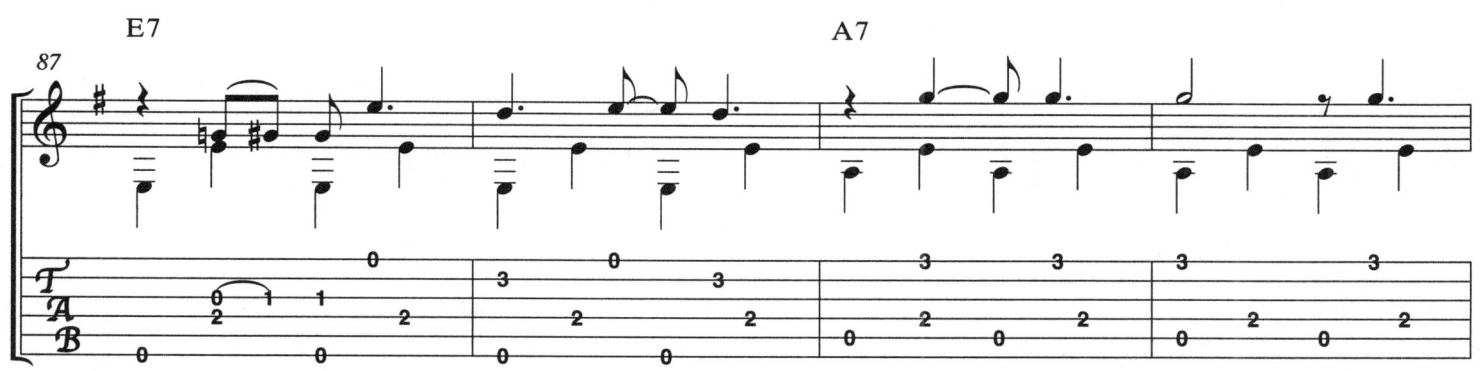
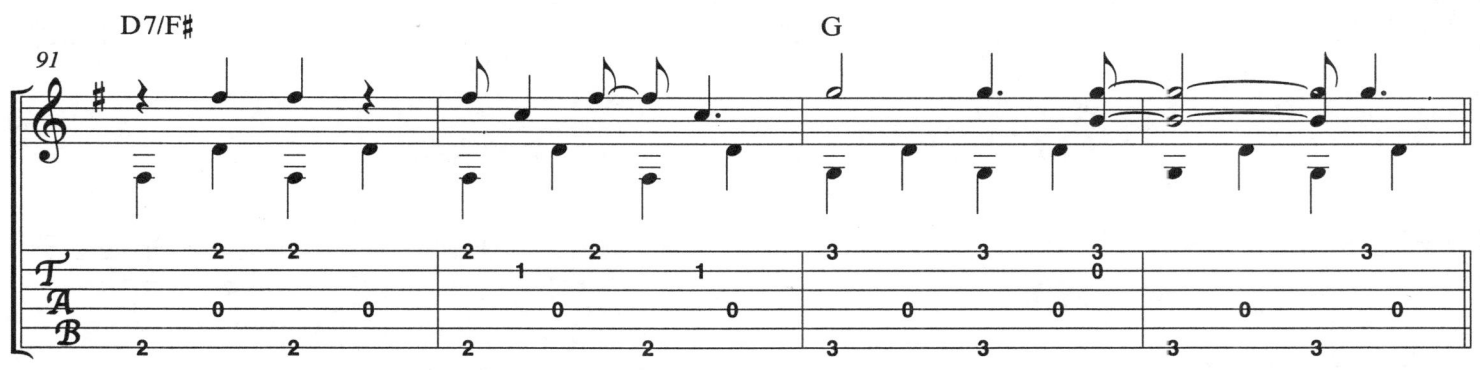
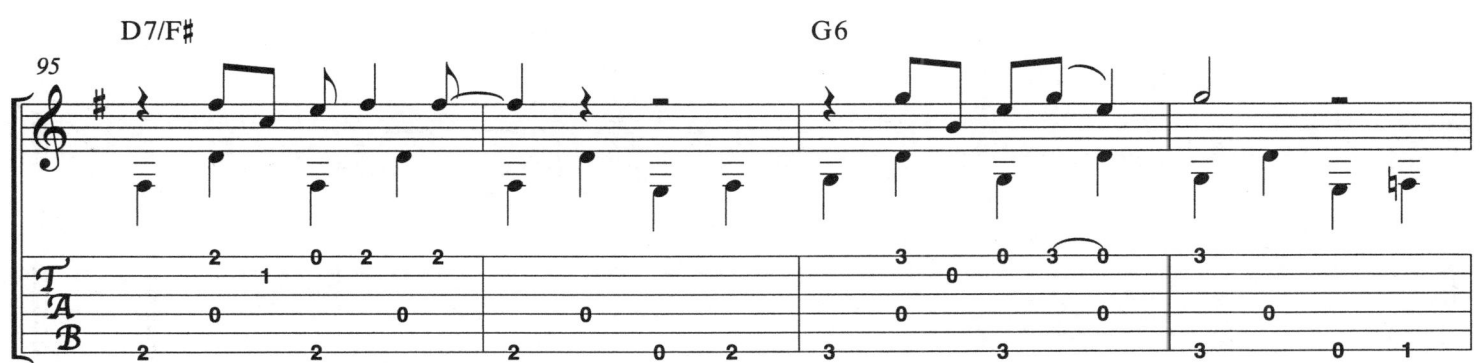

Cascade Rag - 7 - 6
SAIR011

If The Shoe Fits

By KENNY SULTAN

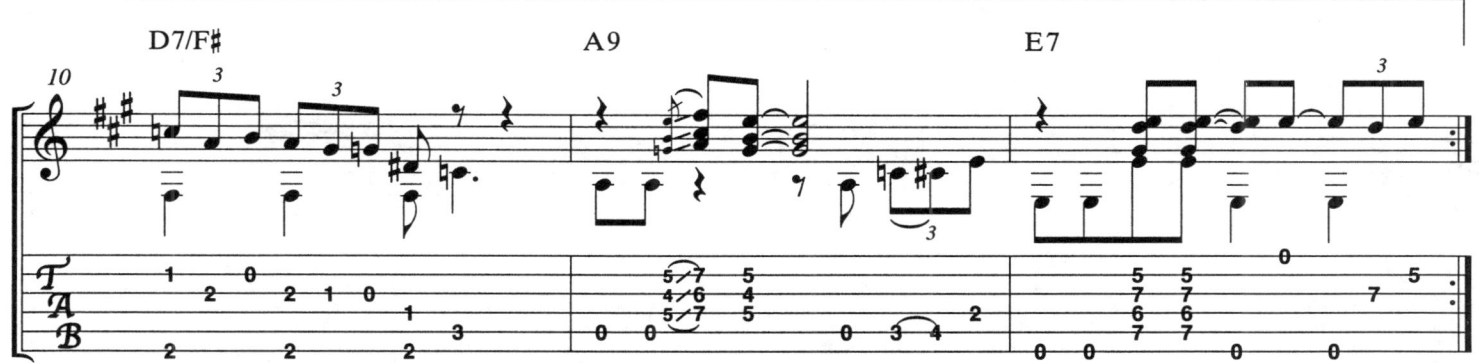

If the Shoe Fits - 5 - 1
SAIR011

© 2002 Original Solid Air Records Music (BMI)
All Rights Reserved

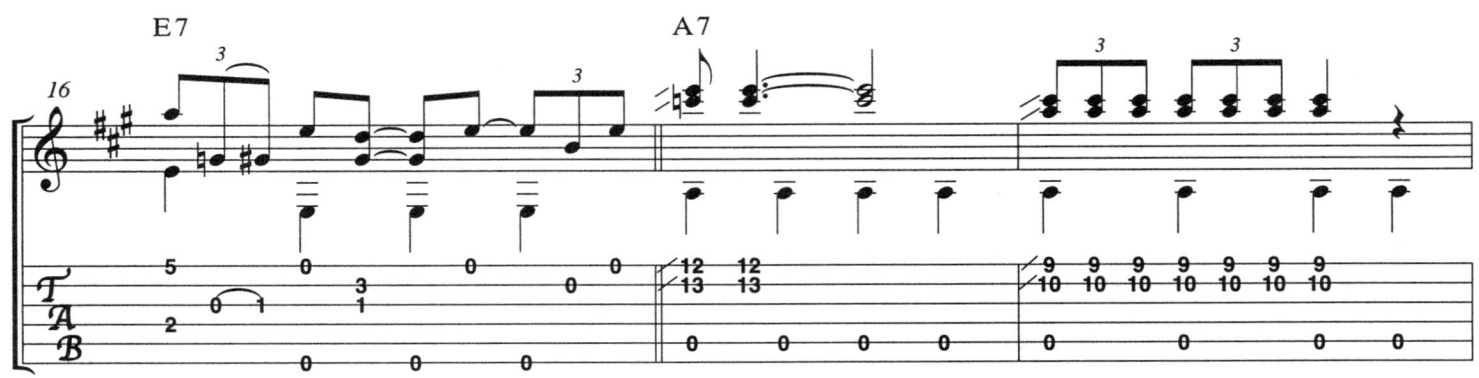
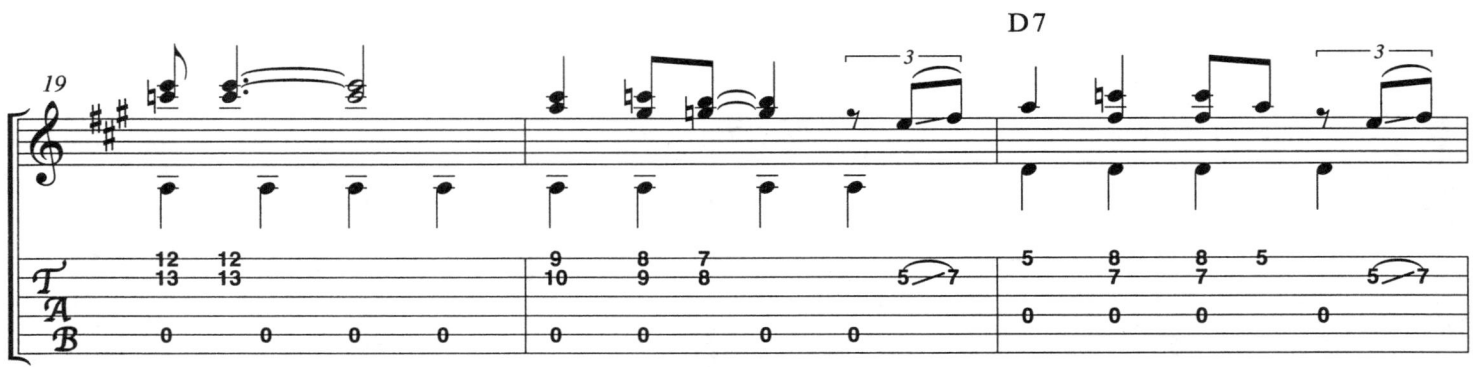
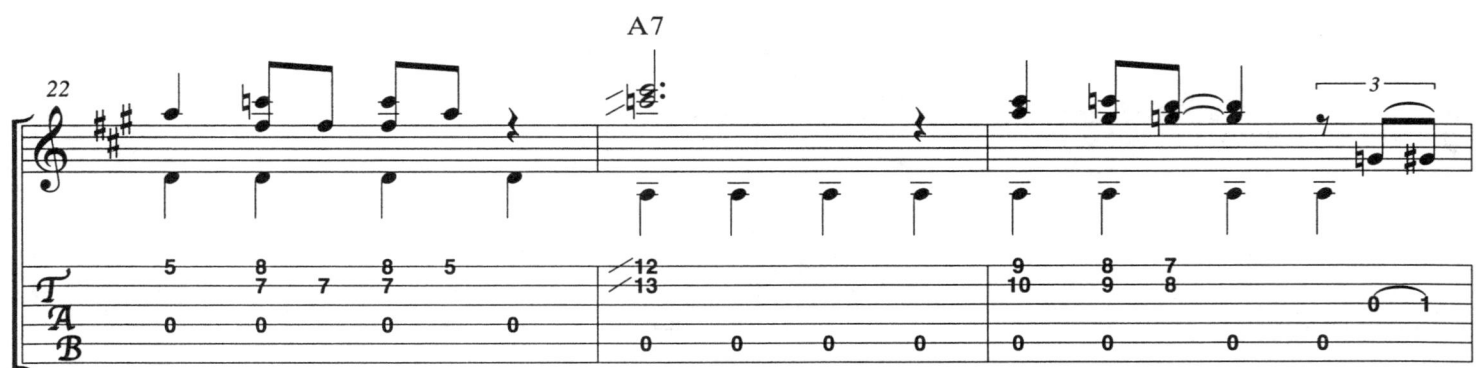

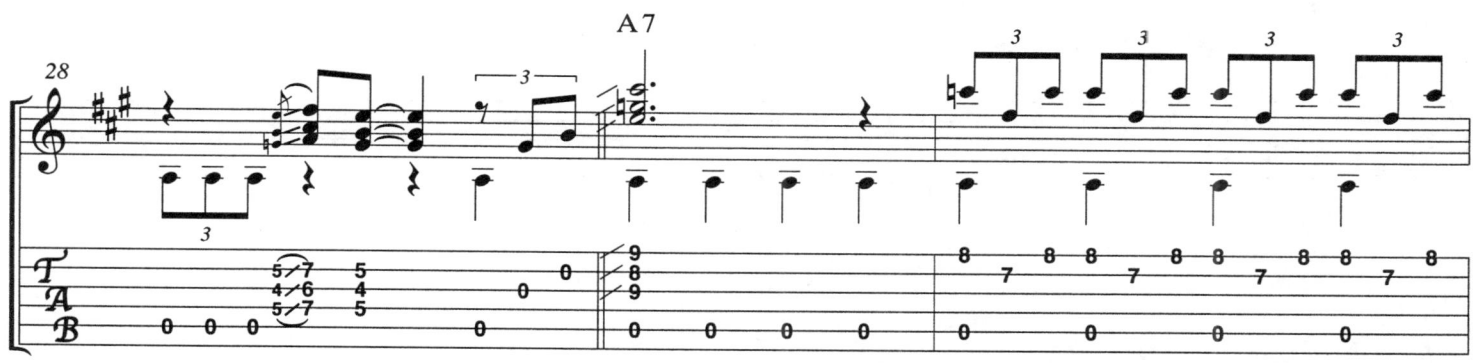
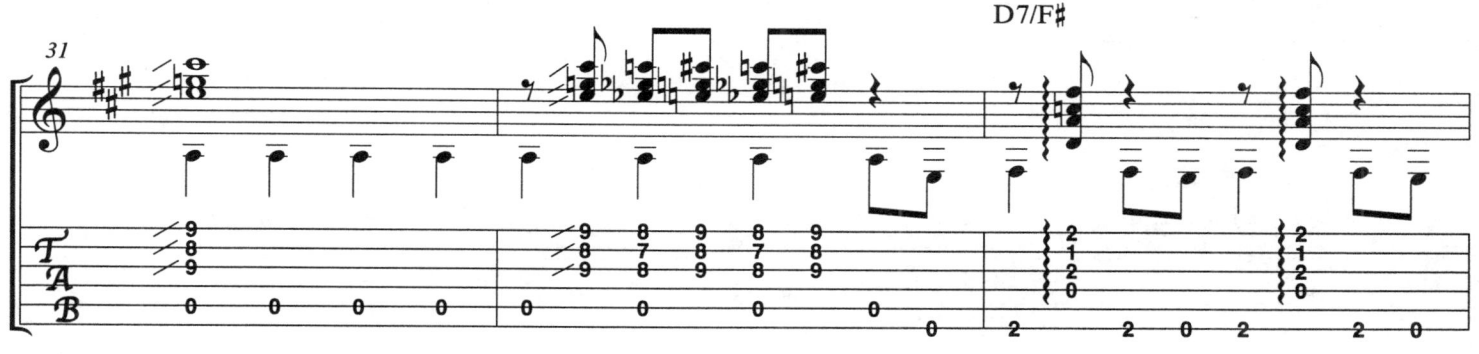
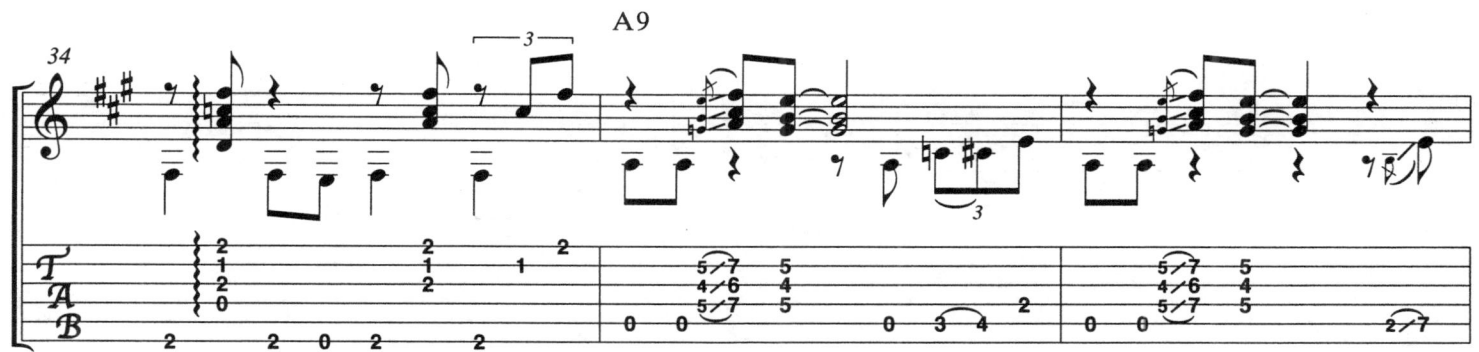

Eureka Hotel

By AL PETTEWAY

Tune to DADGAD, Capo 2:
⑥ = D ③ = G
⑤ = A ② = A
④ = D ① = D

Moderately ♩ = 95

*Recording sounds a whole step higher than written.

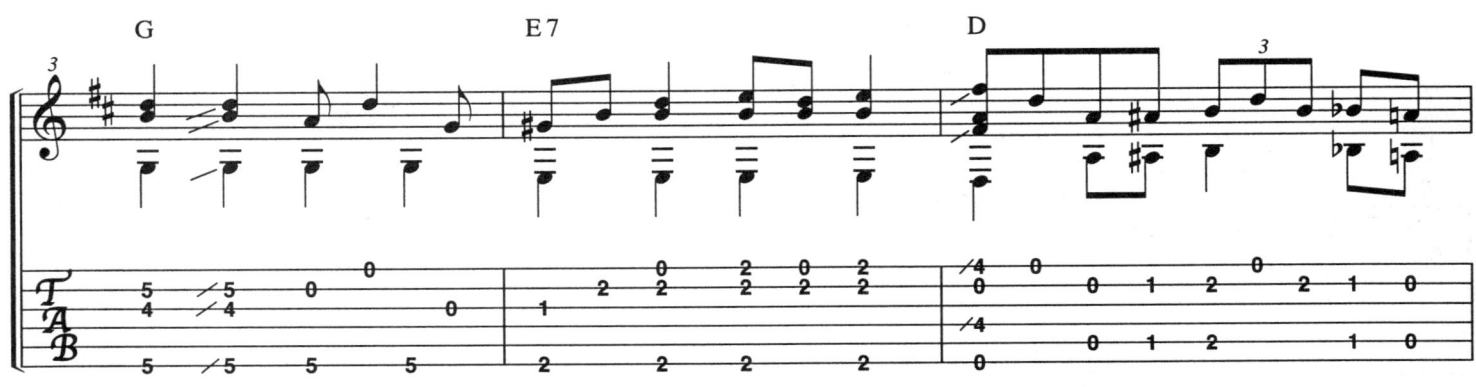

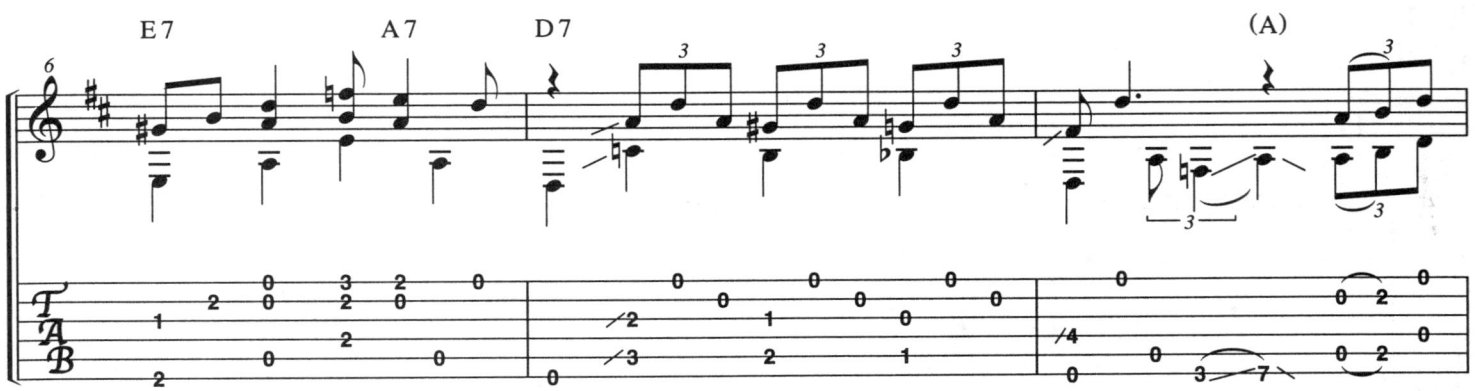

Eureka Hotel - 6 - 1
SAIR011

© 2002 Al Petteway (BMI)
All Rights Reserved

25

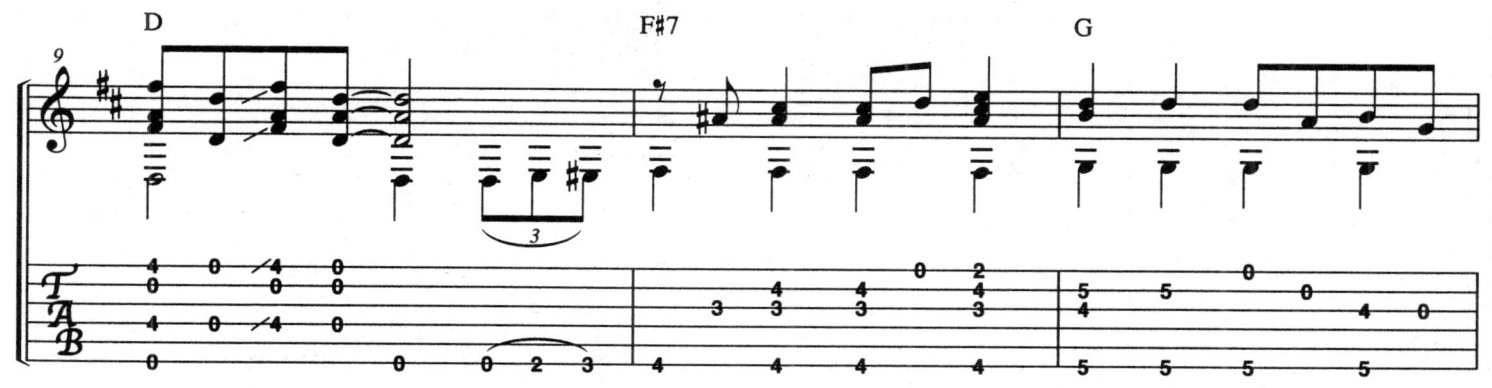

Eureka Hotel - 6 - 2
SAIR011

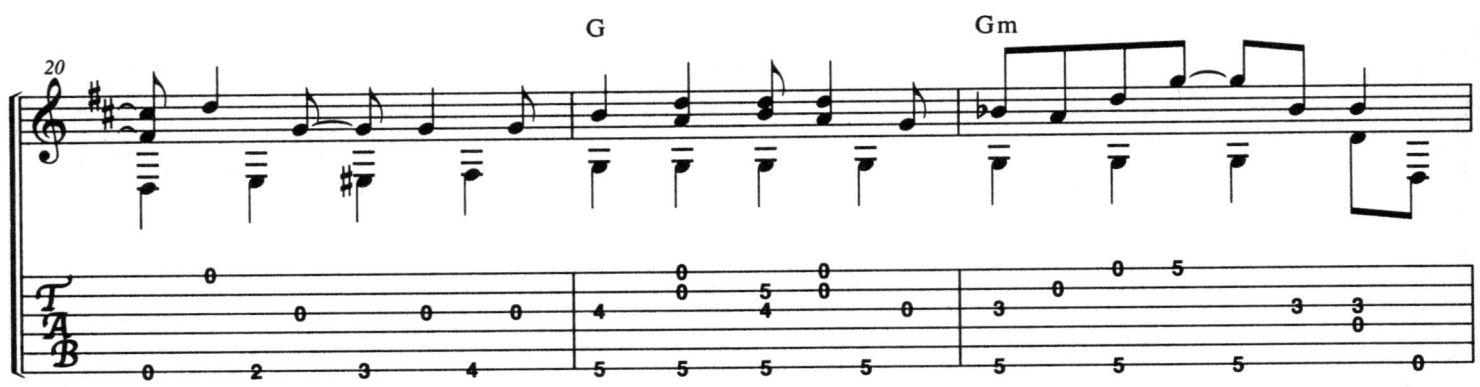
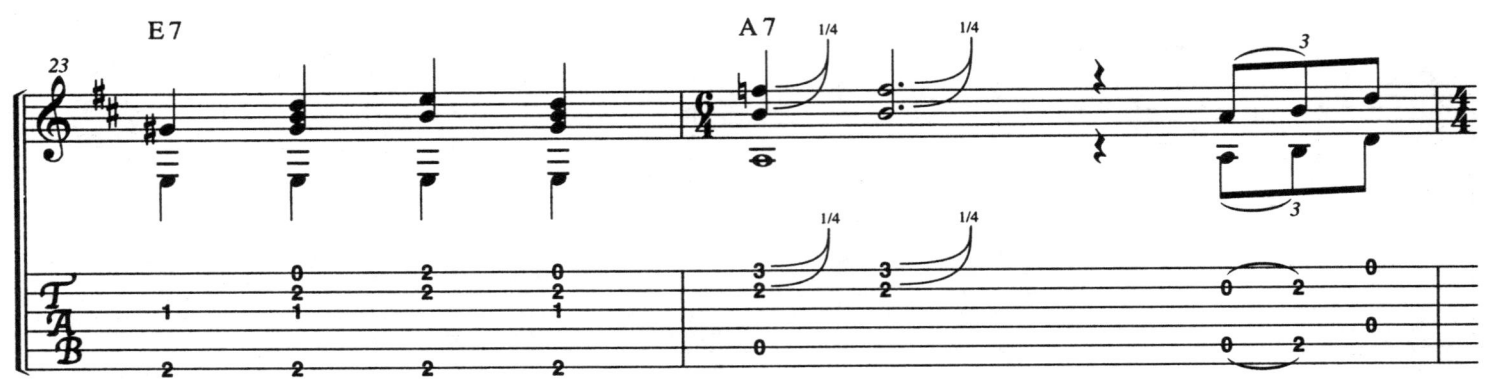
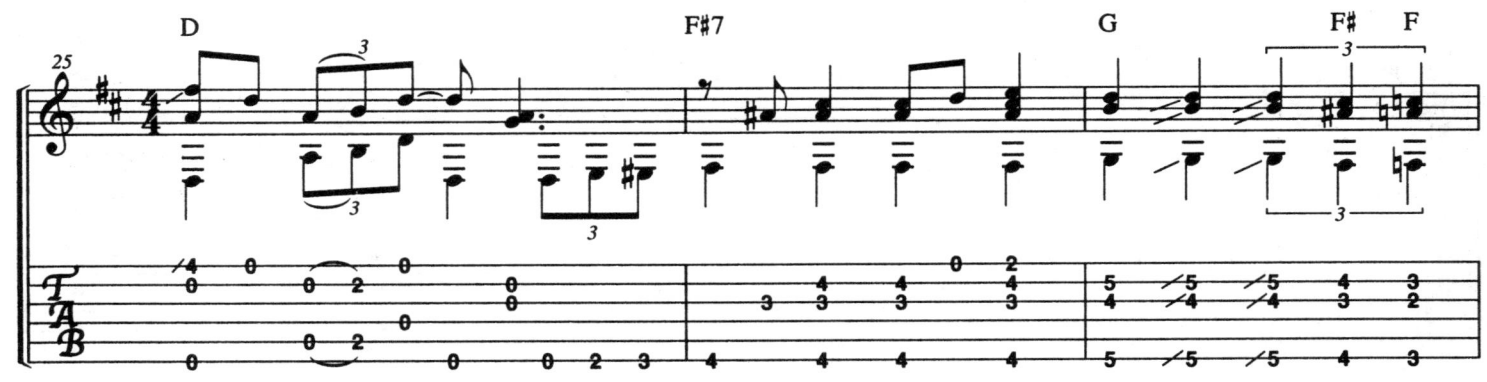
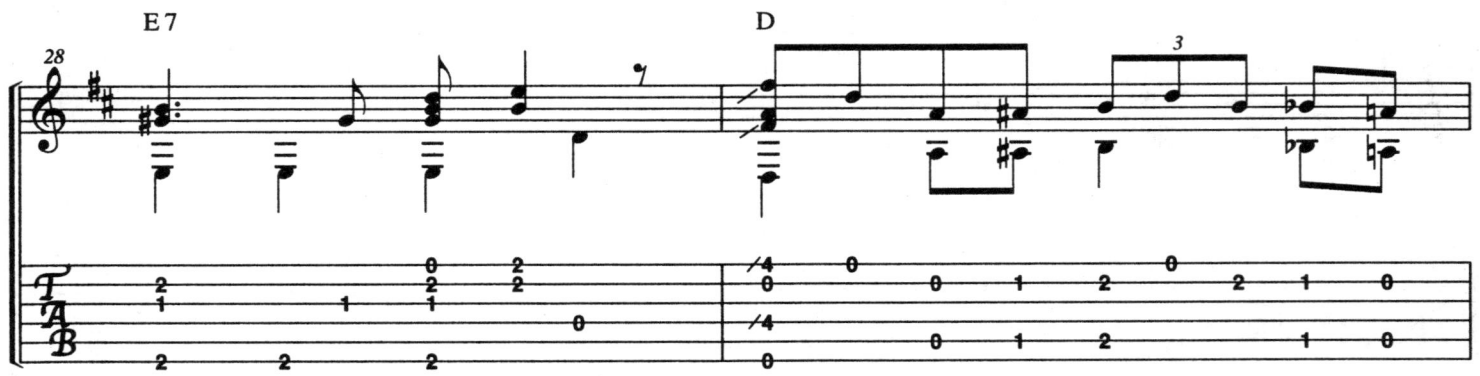

27

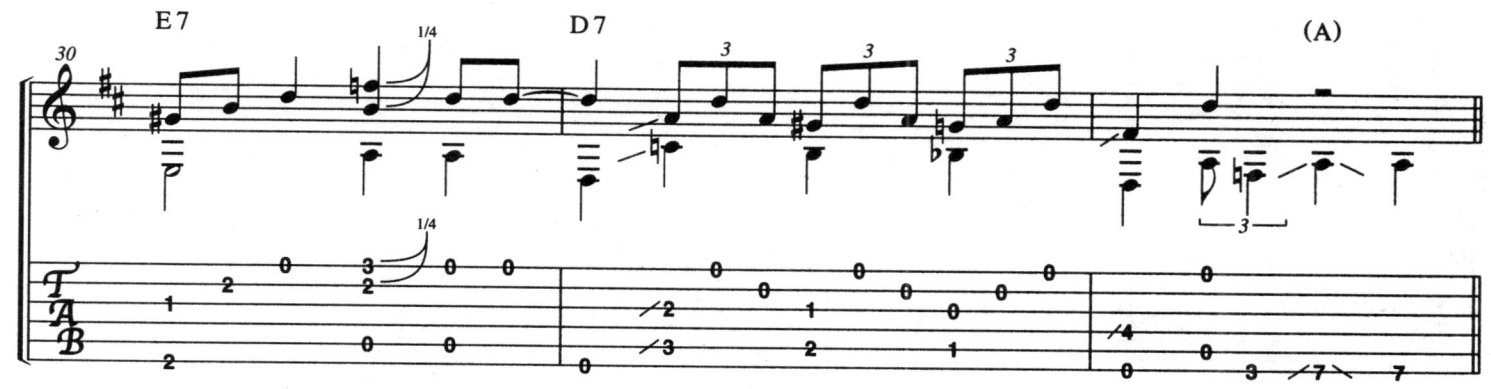
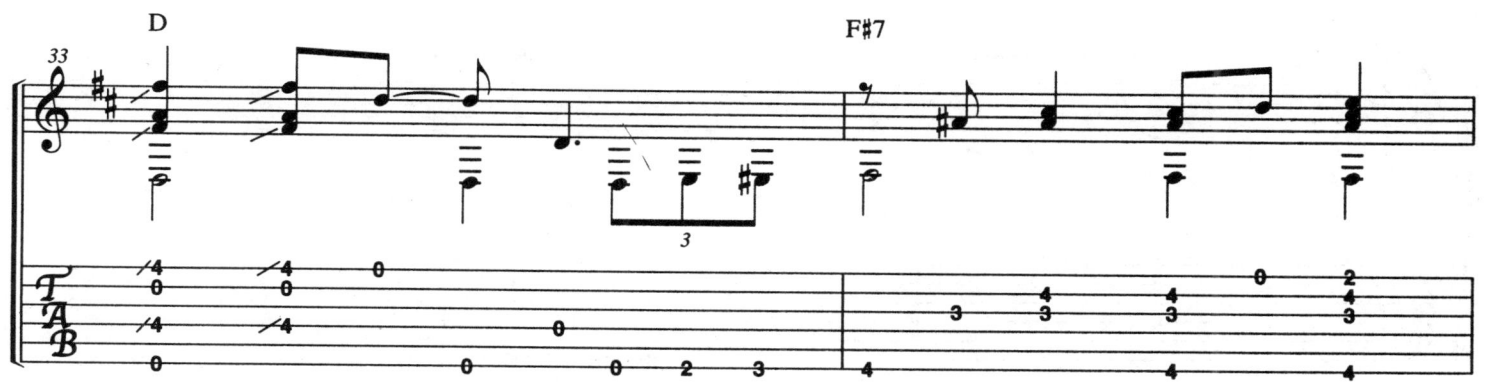

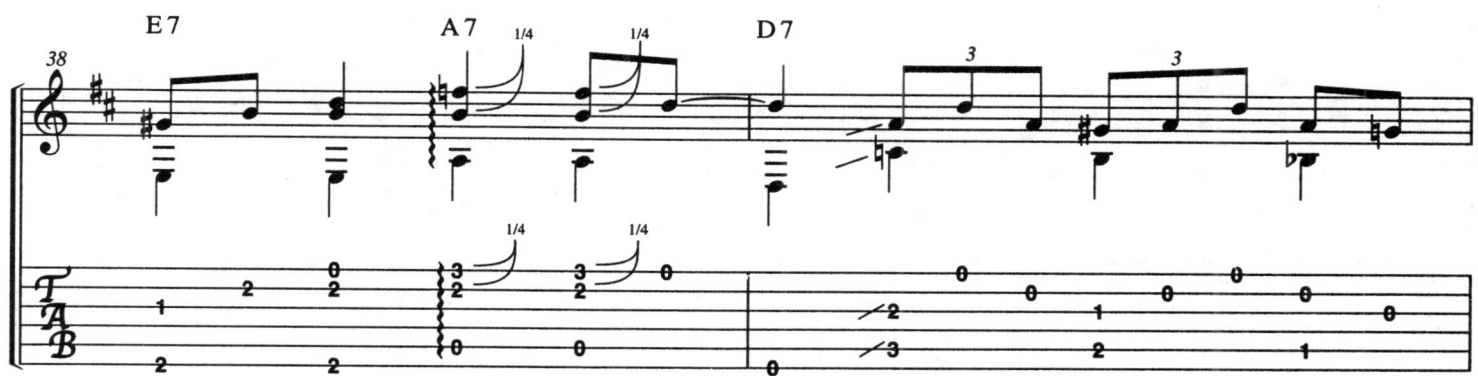

Eureka Hotel - 6 - 4
SAIR011

28

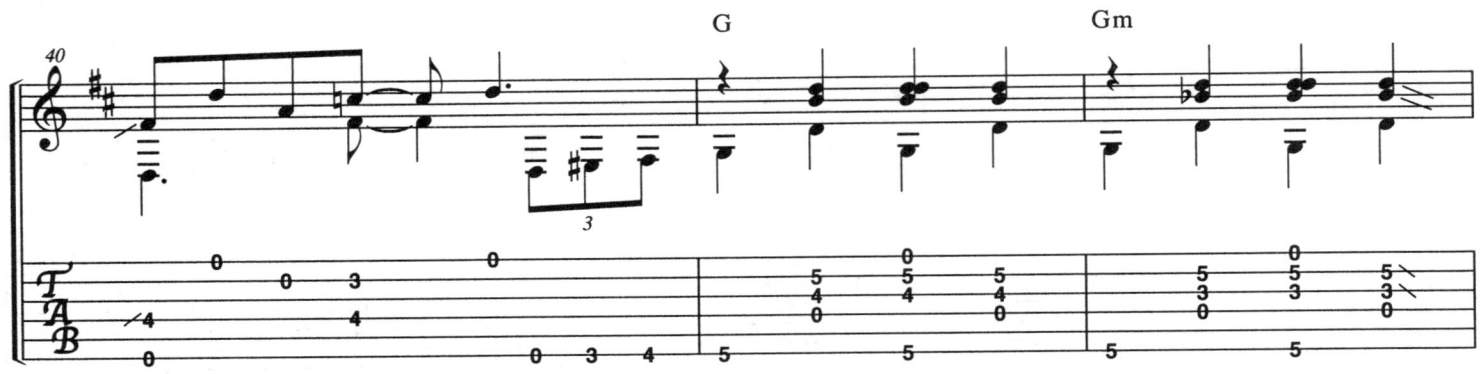

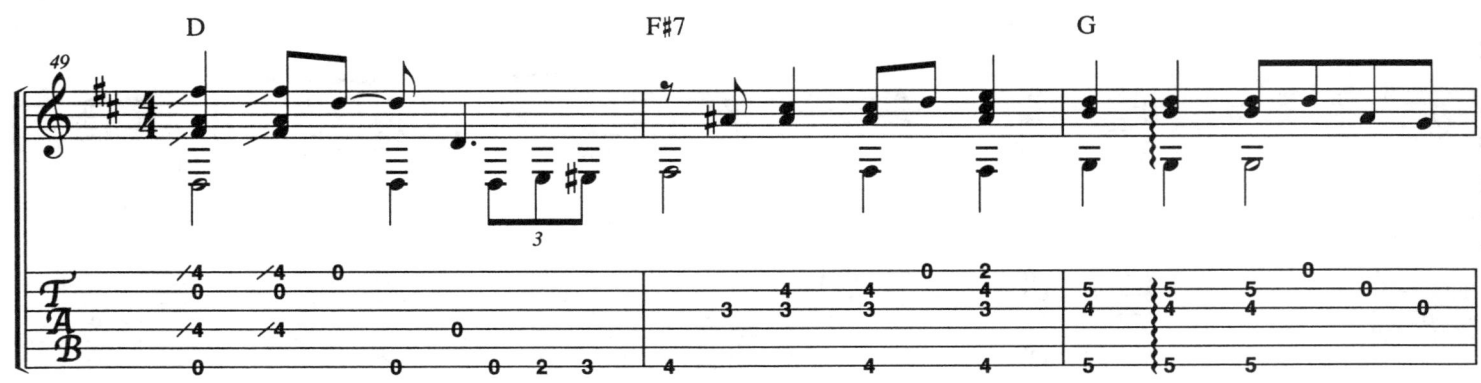

Eureka Hotel - 6 - 5
SAIR011

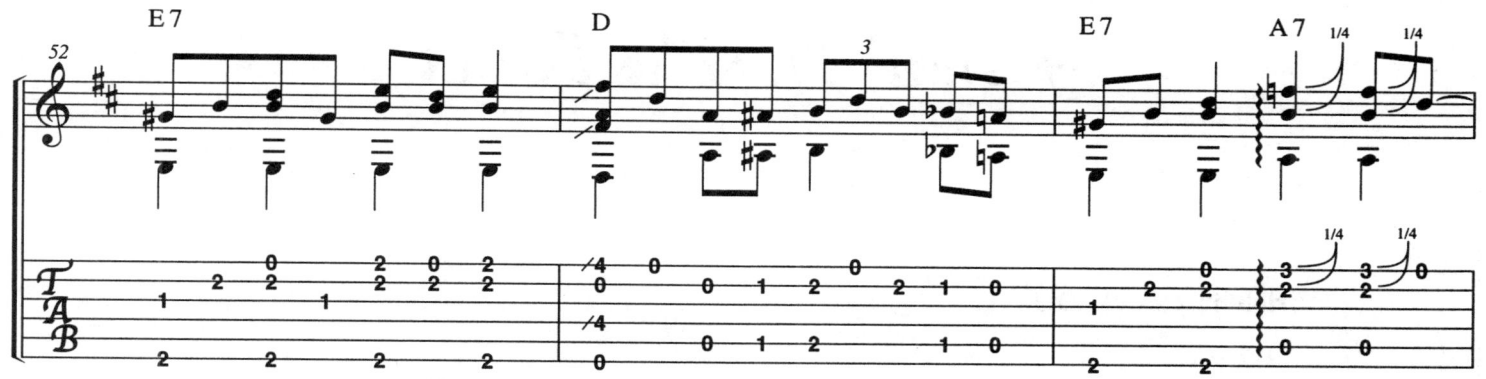

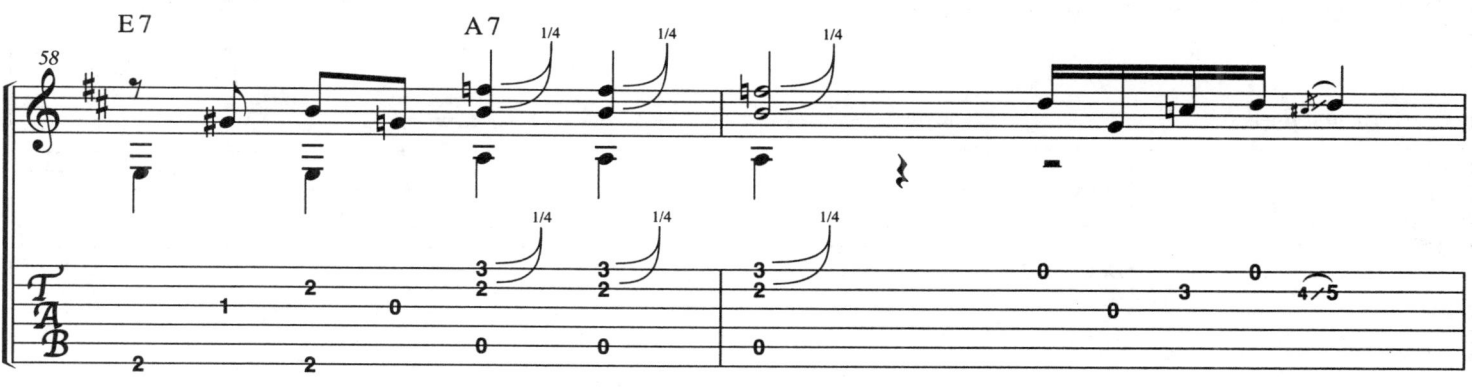
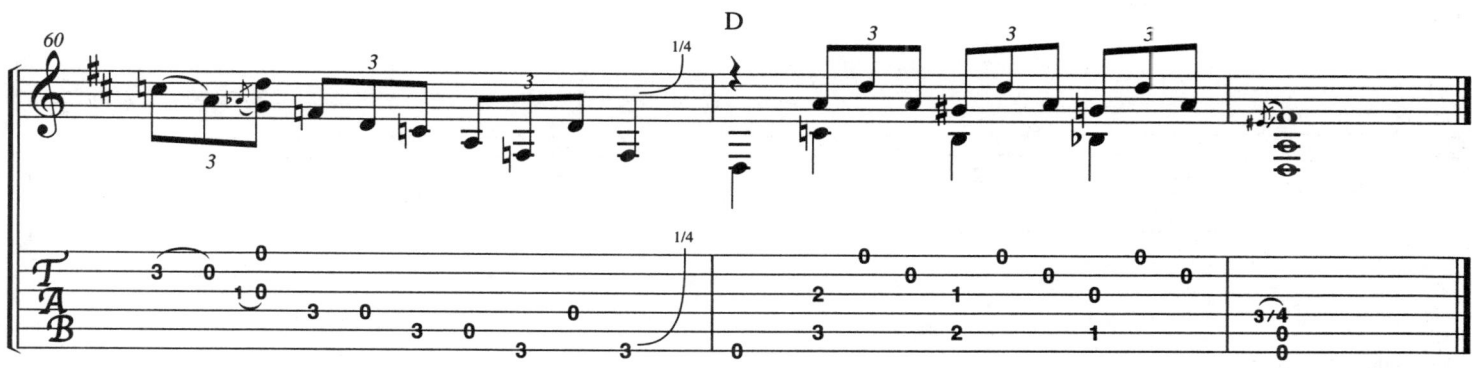

Fishin' In The Wind

By MIKE DOWLING

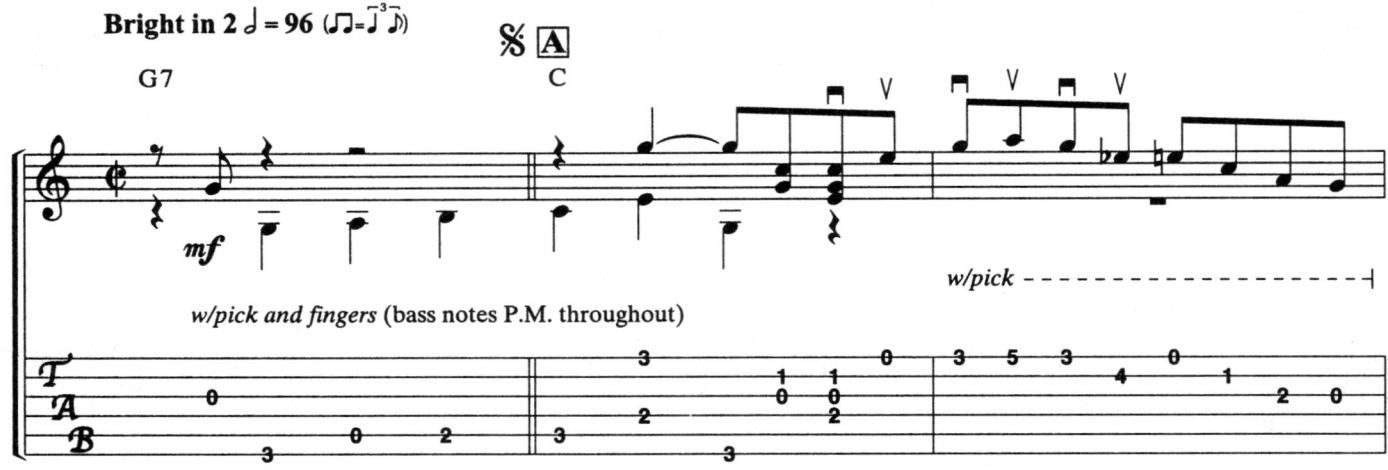

*Down stroke w/pick.

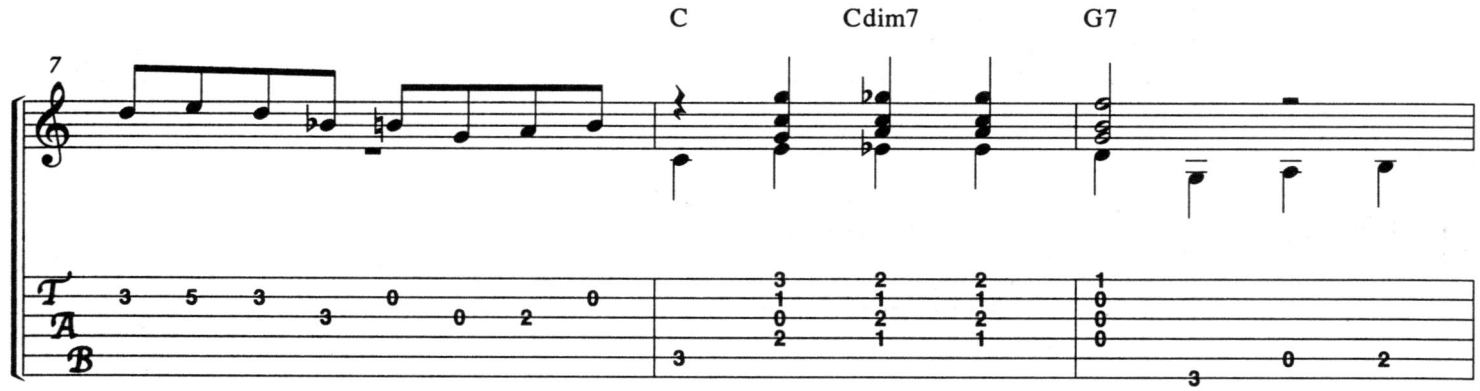

Fishin' in the Wind - 6 - 1
SAIR011

© 2001 TableTop Music (ASCAP) and Solid Air Music (ASCAP)
All Rights Reserved

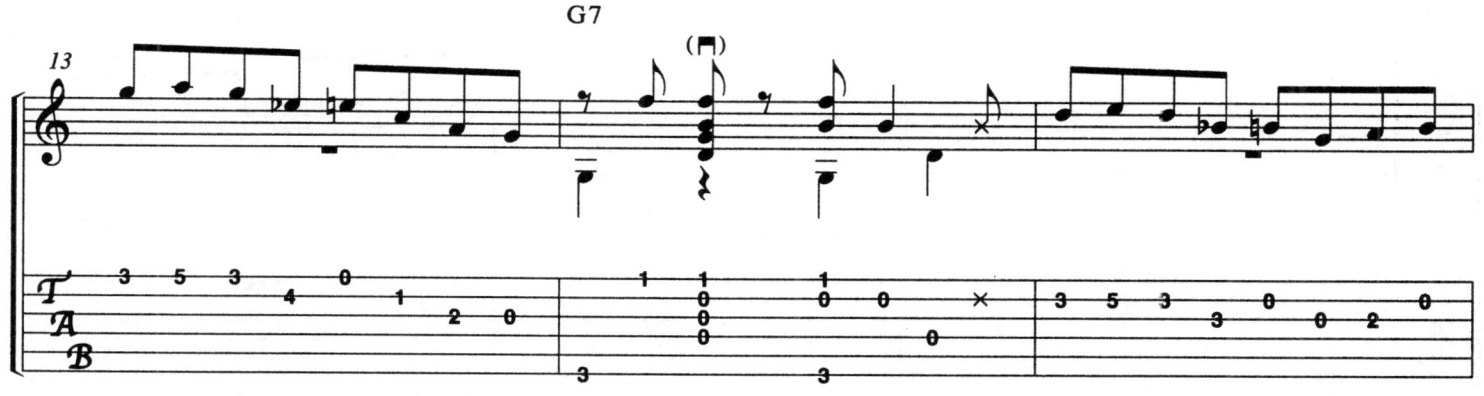
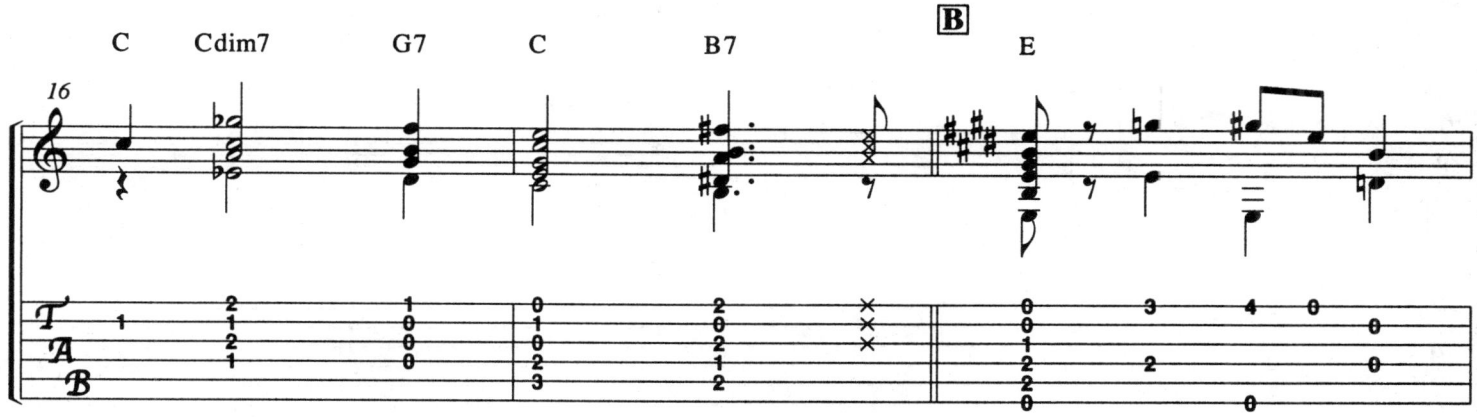
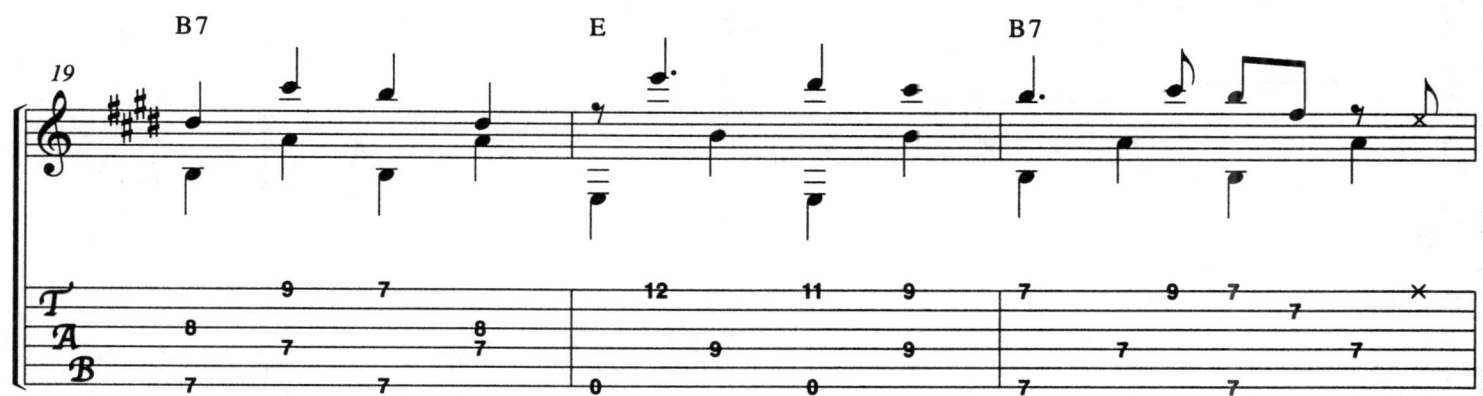

Fishin' in the Wind - 6 - 2
SAIR011

32

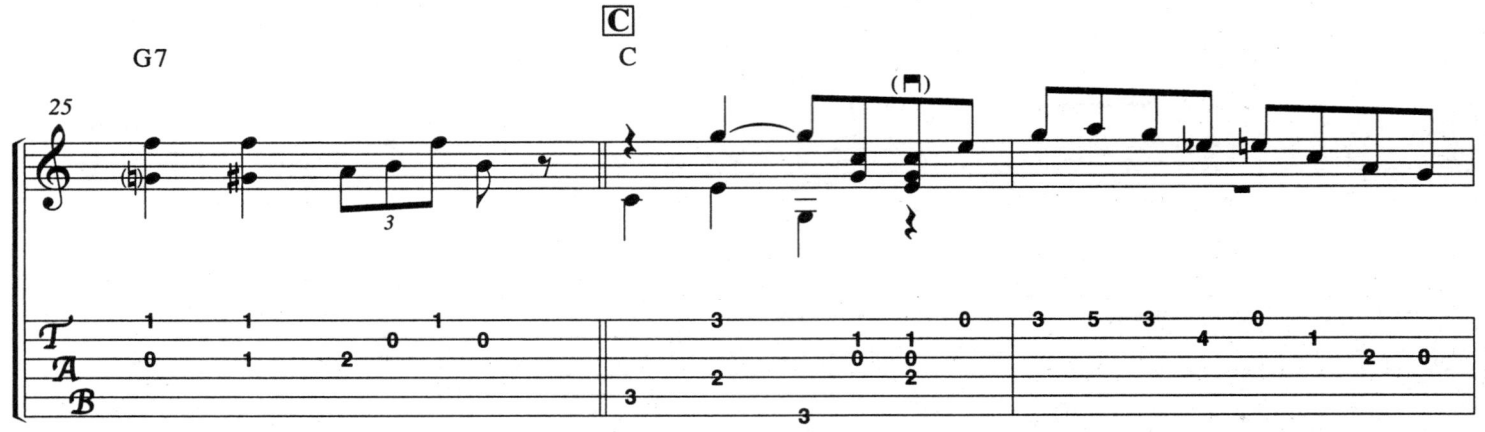

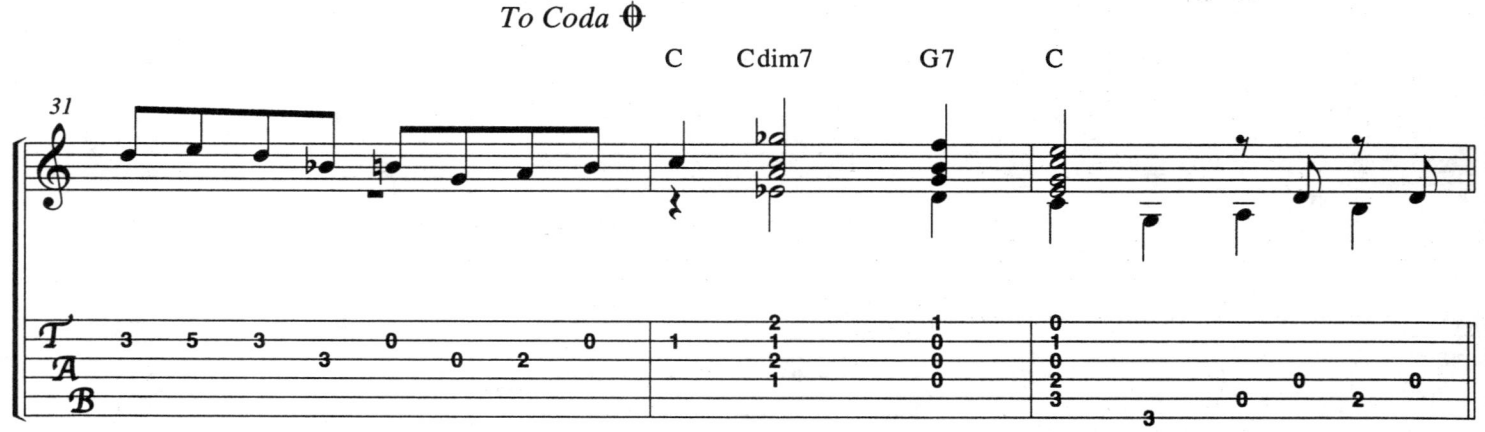

Fishin' in the Wind - 6 - 3
SAIR011

33

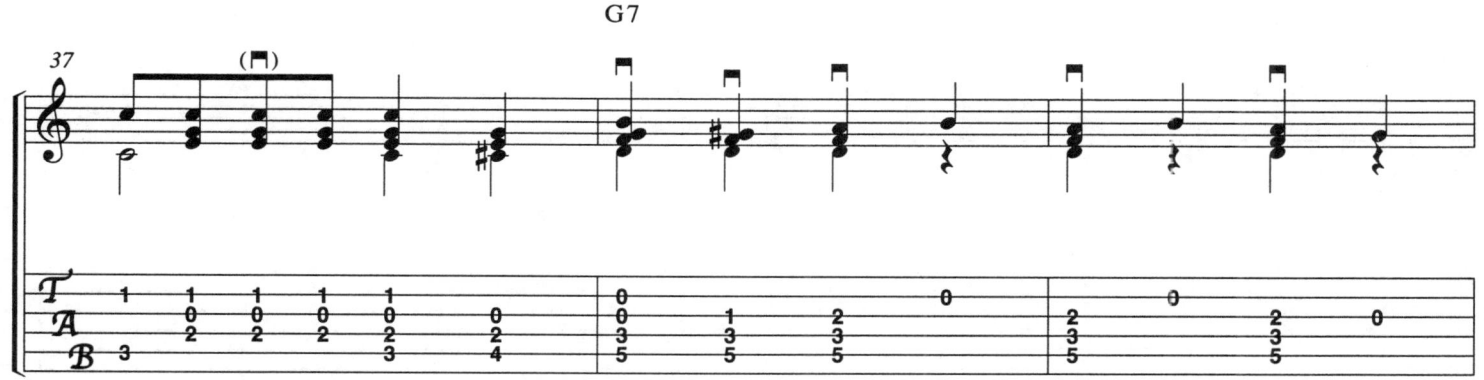

Fishin' in the Wind - 6 - 4
SAIR011

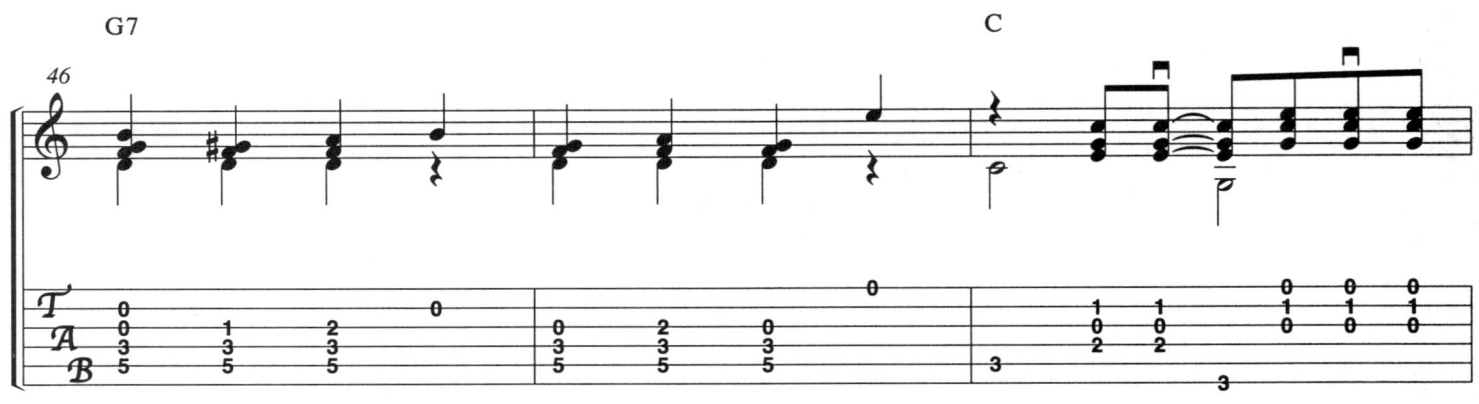
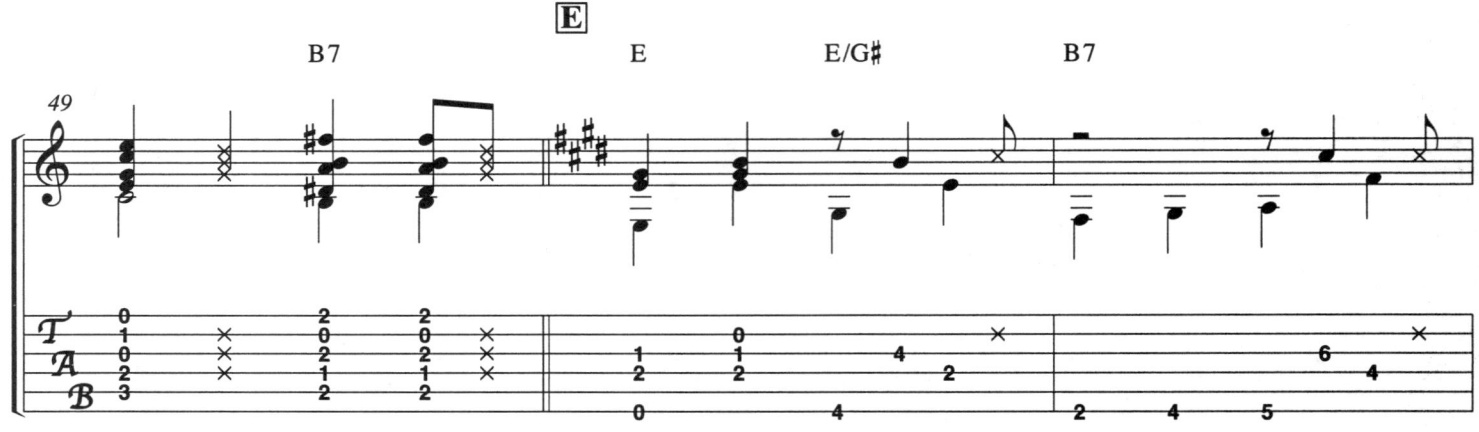
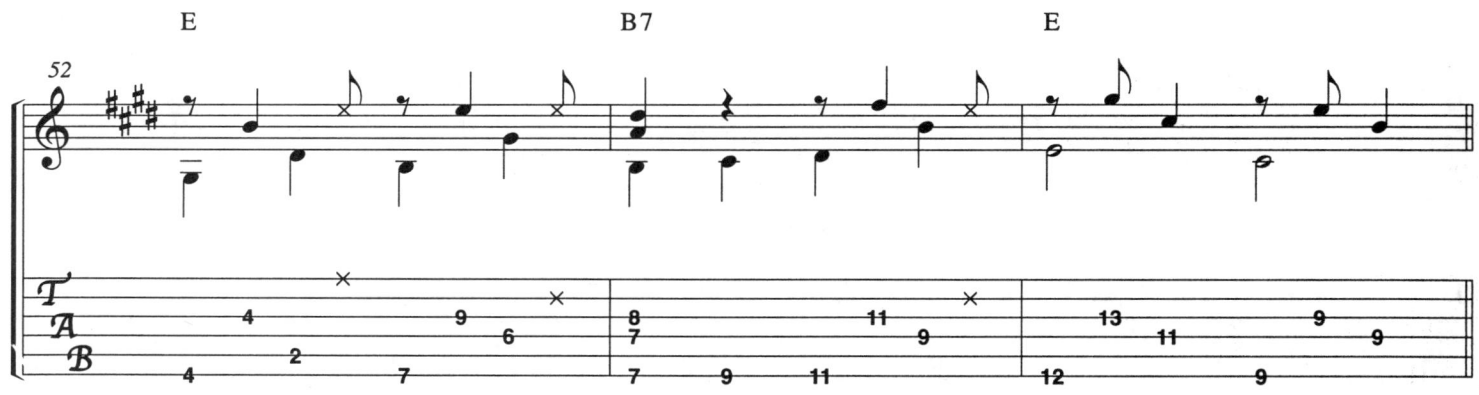
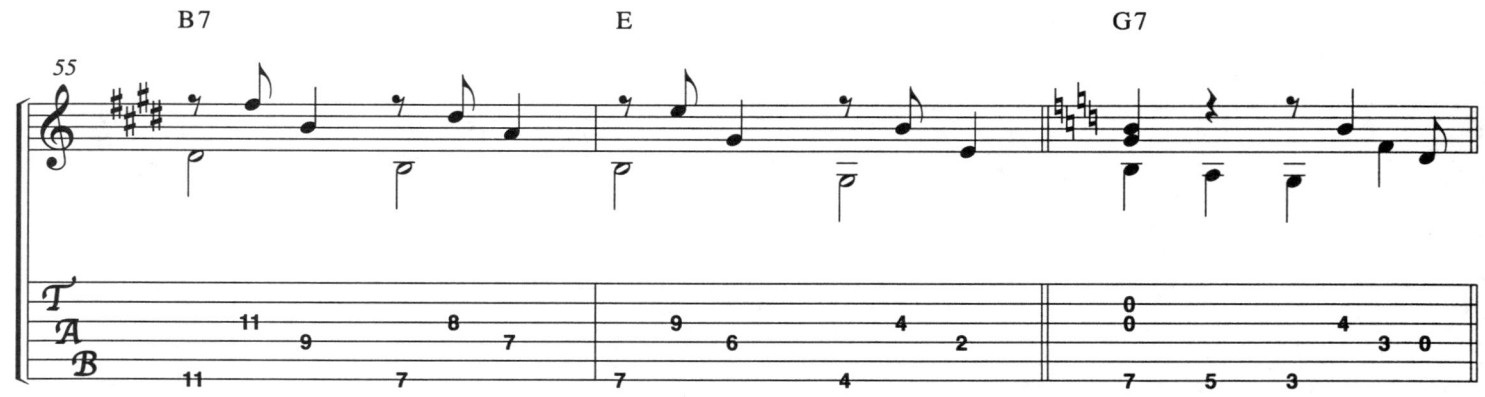

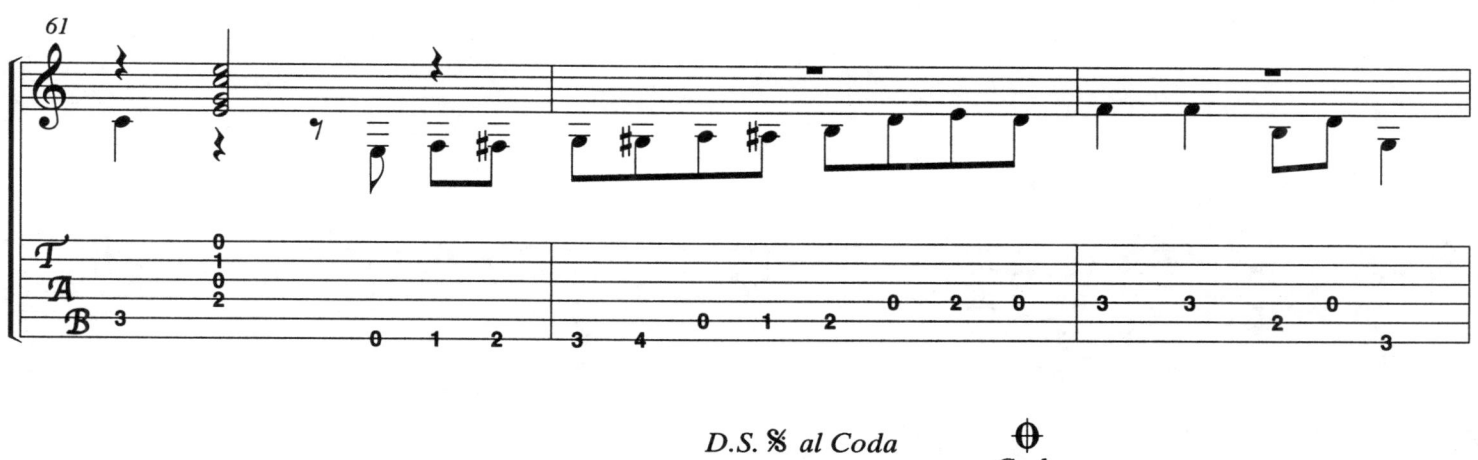

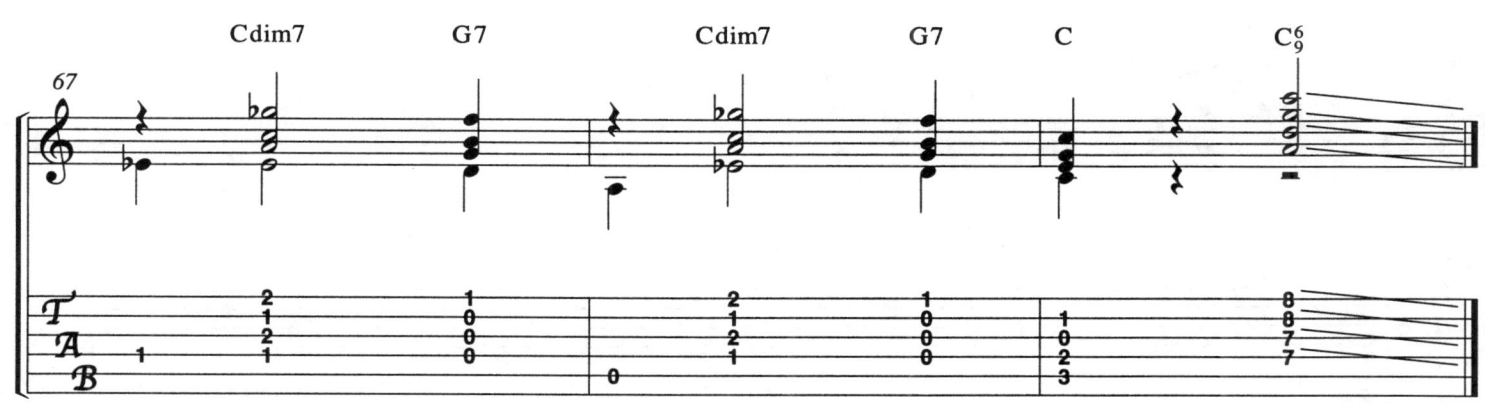

Fishin' in the Wind - 6 - 6
SAIR011

Honky Tonk

By KENNY SULTAN

Moderate shuffle ♩ = 125

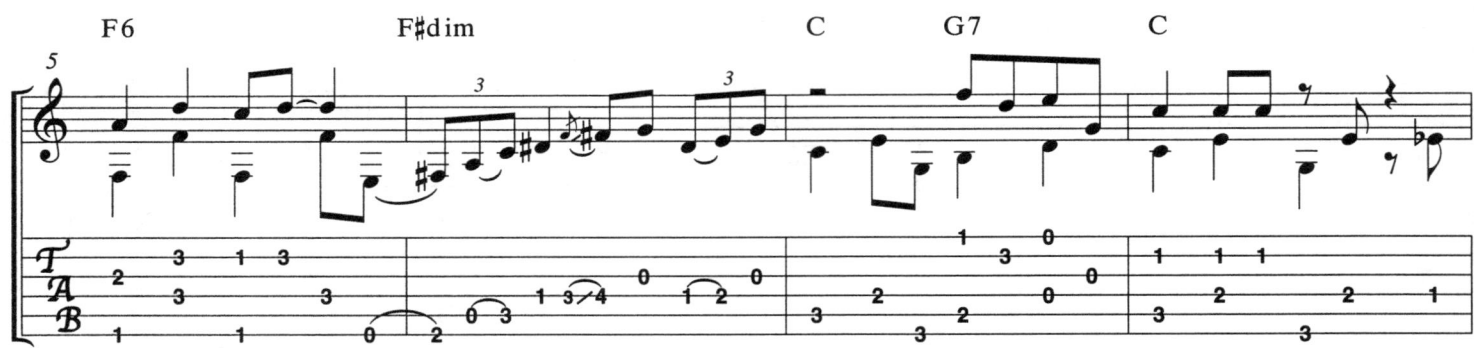

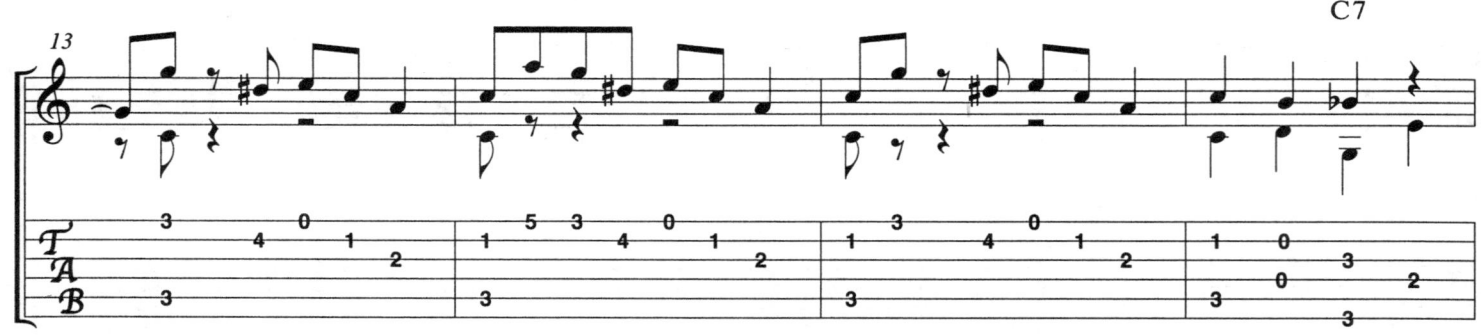

Honky Tonk - 6 - 1
SAIR011

© 2001 Good Times Music (BMI) and Original Solid Air Records Music (BMI)
All Rights Reserved

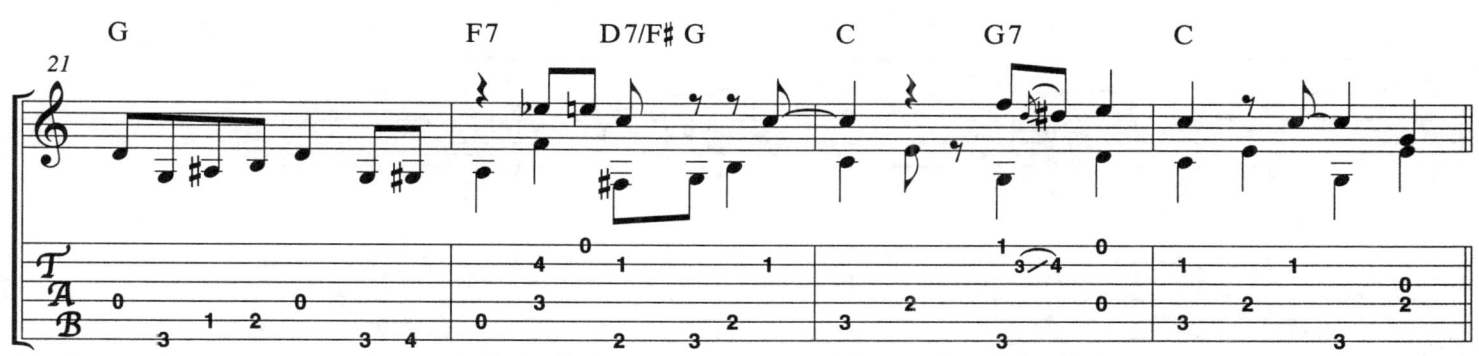

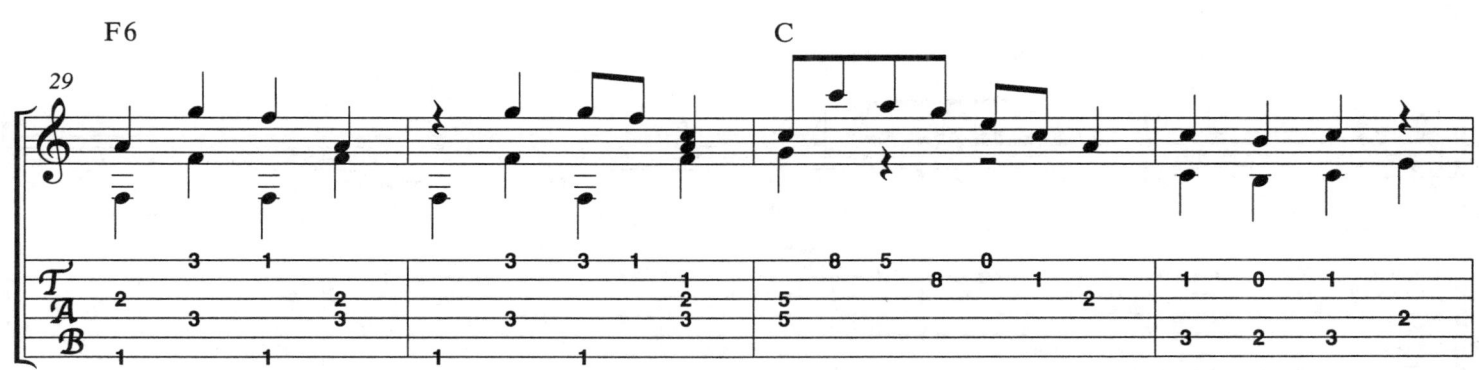

38

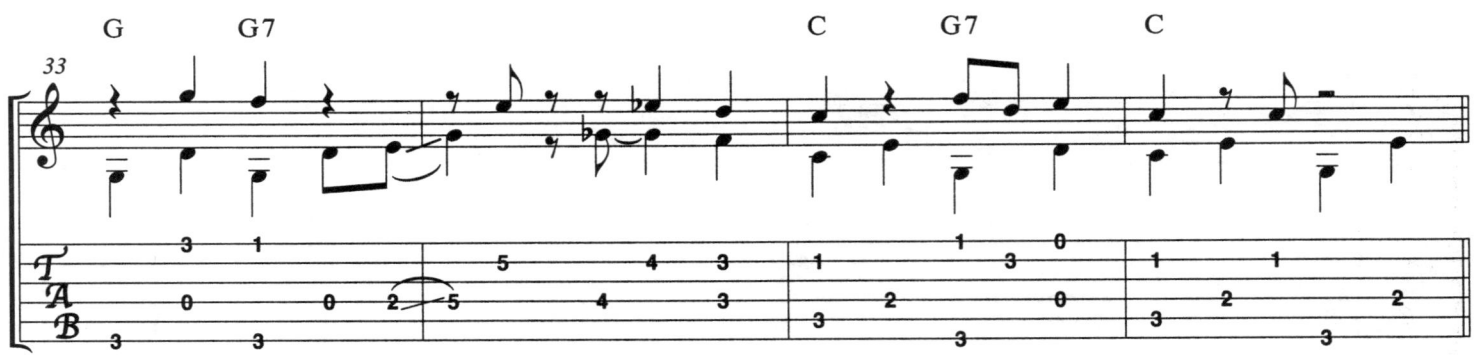
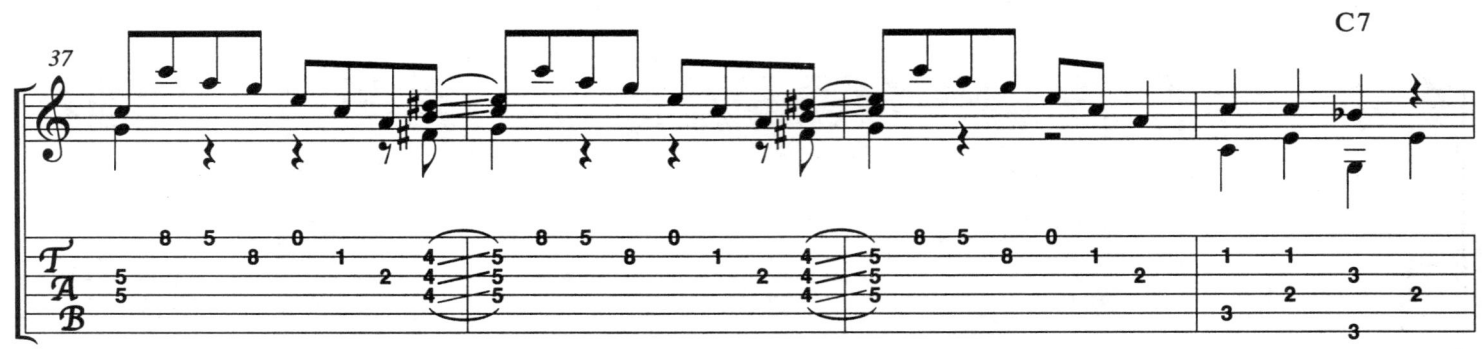
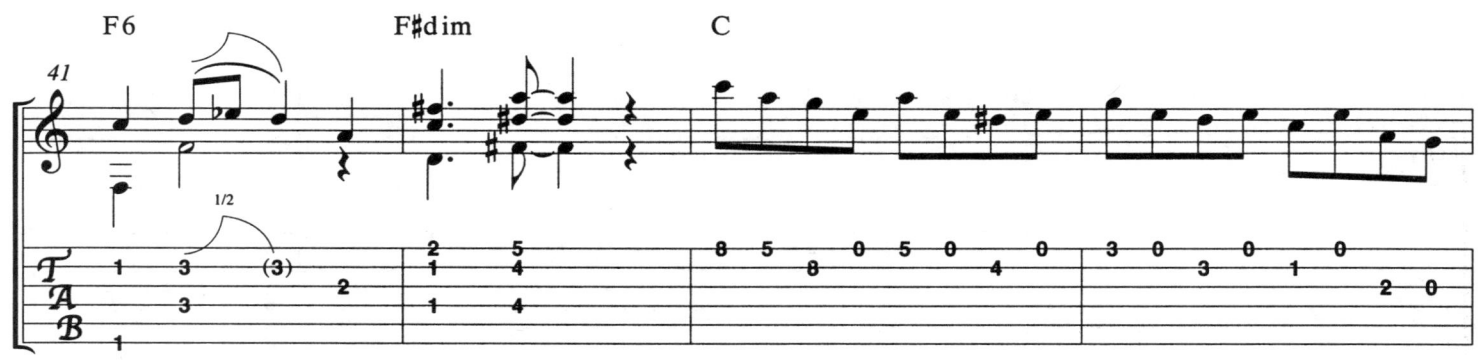

Honky Tonk - 6 - 3
SAIR011

39

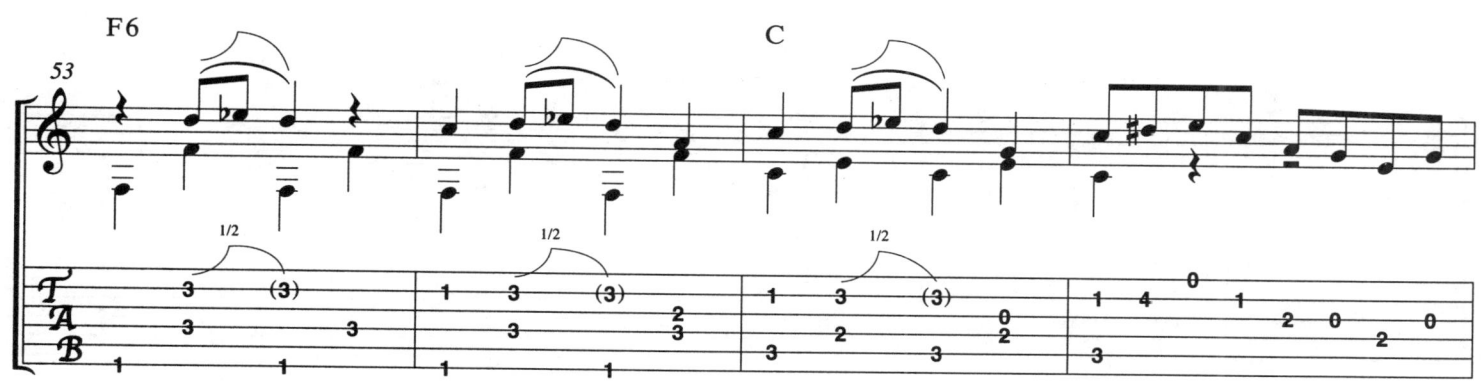

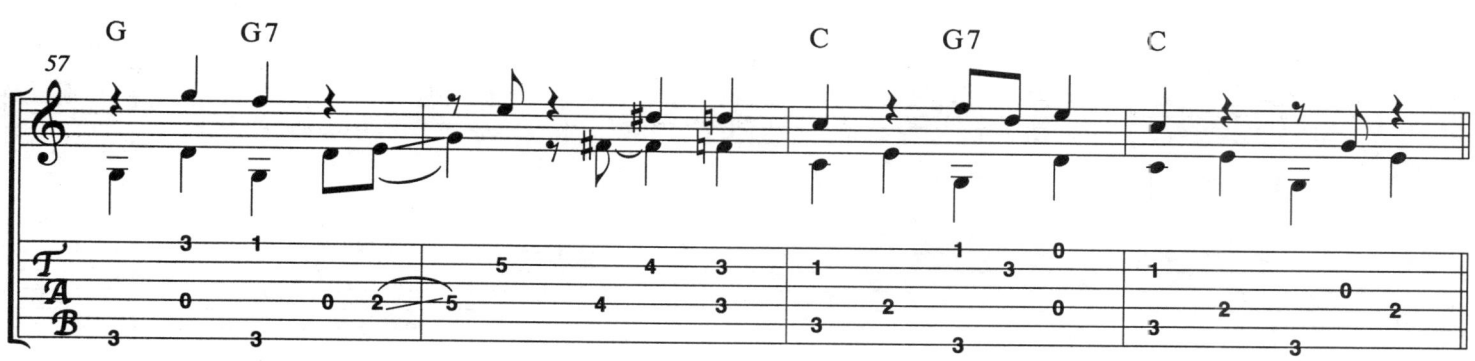

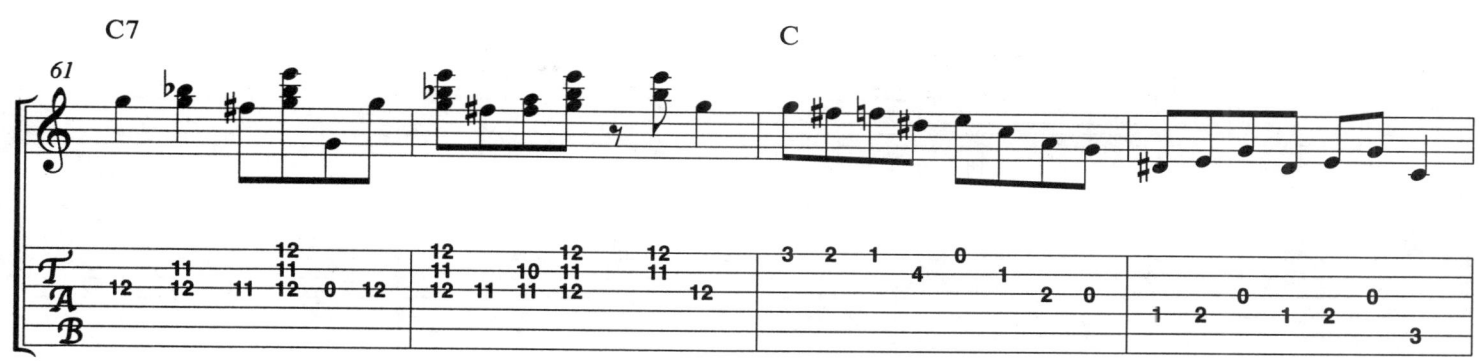

Honky Tonk - 6 - 4
SAIR011

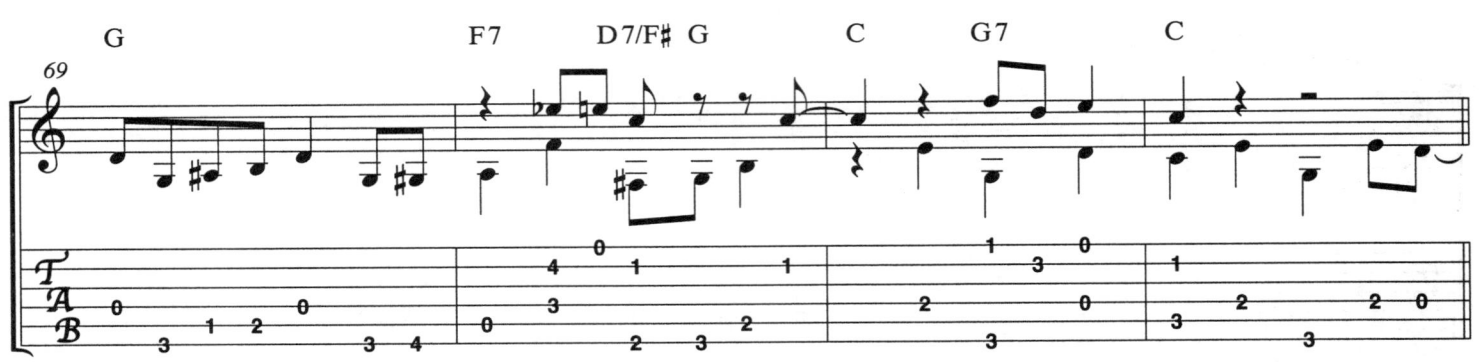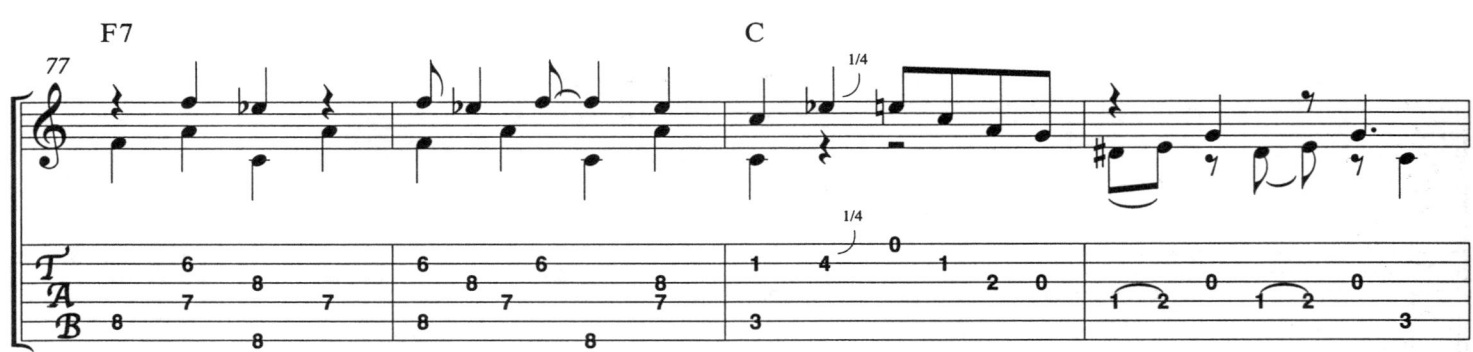

Johnson City Rag

By MIKE DOWLING

Standard tuning

44

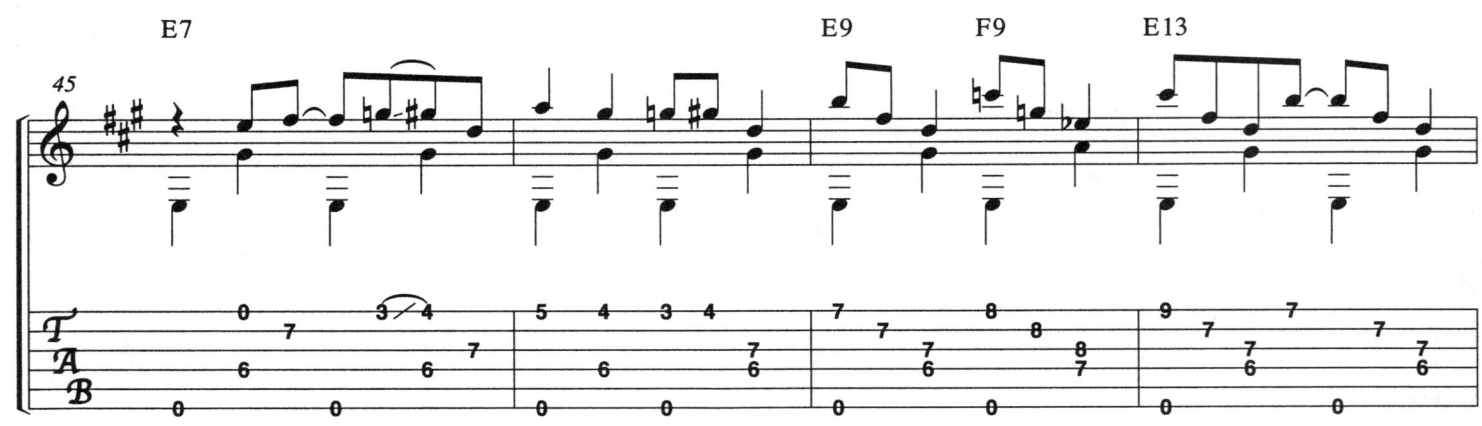

Johnson City Rag - 7 - 3
SAIR011

Johnson City Rag - 7 - 5
SAIR011

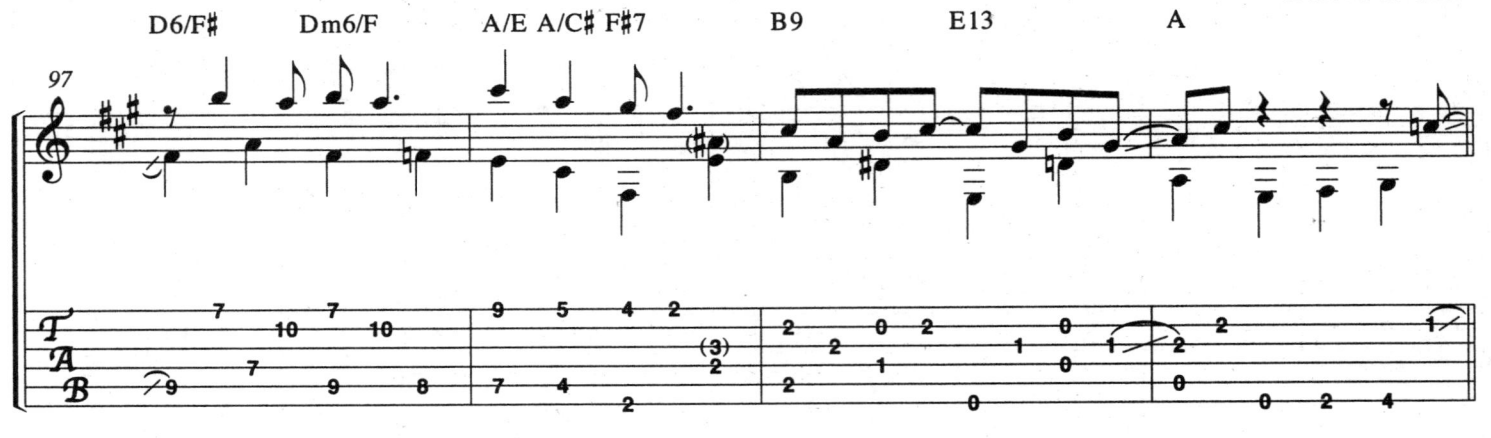
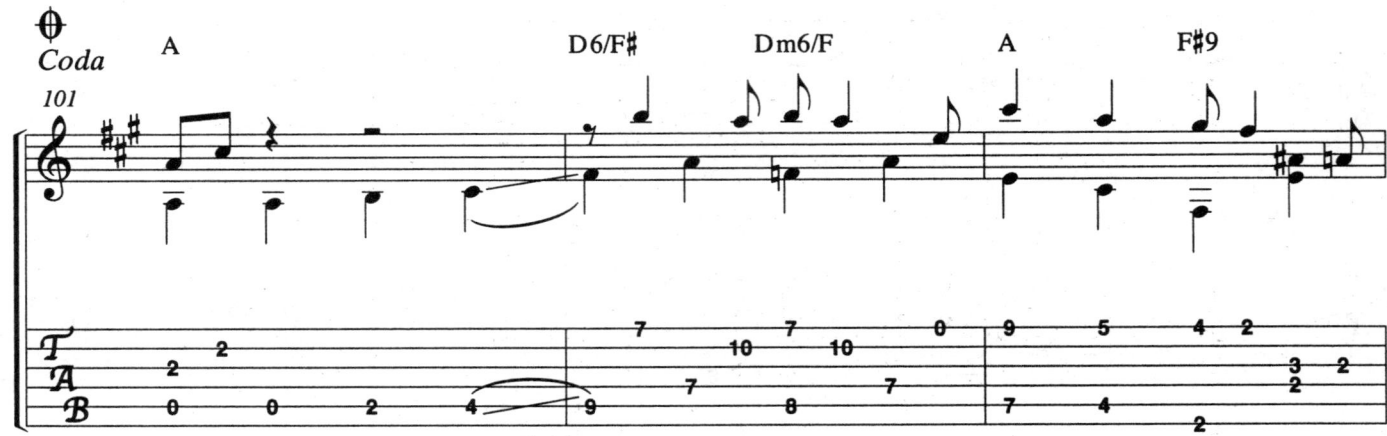
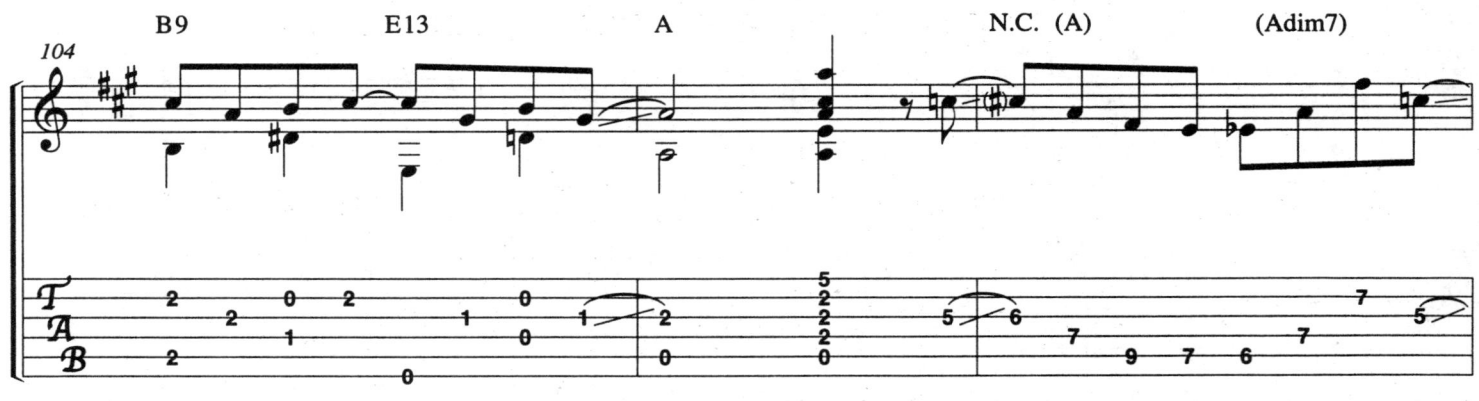
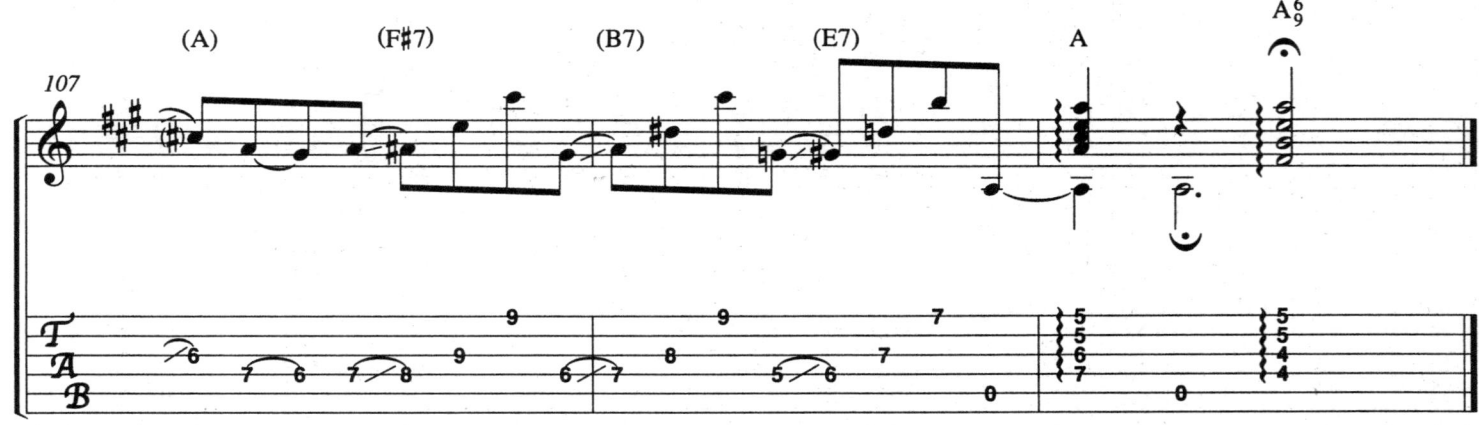

Johnson City Rag - 7 - 7
SAIR011

Lightnin' Strikes

By KENNY SULTAN

Medium fast shuffle ♩ = 130

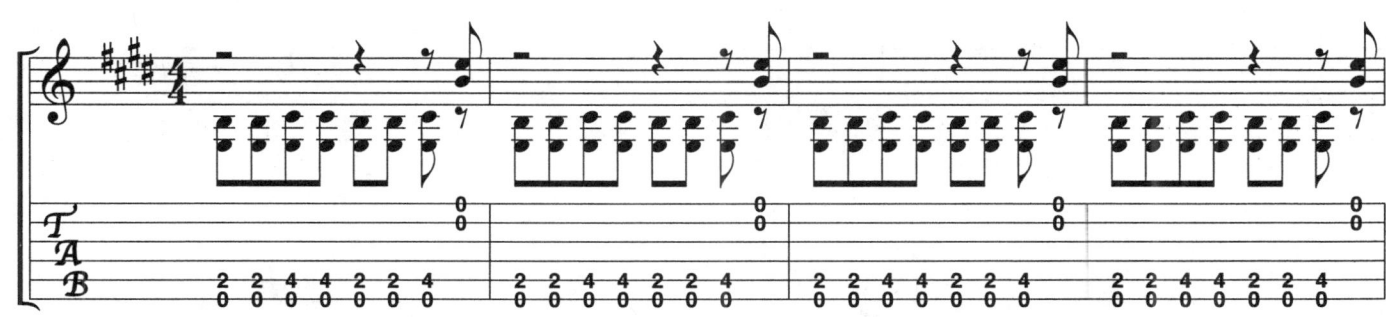
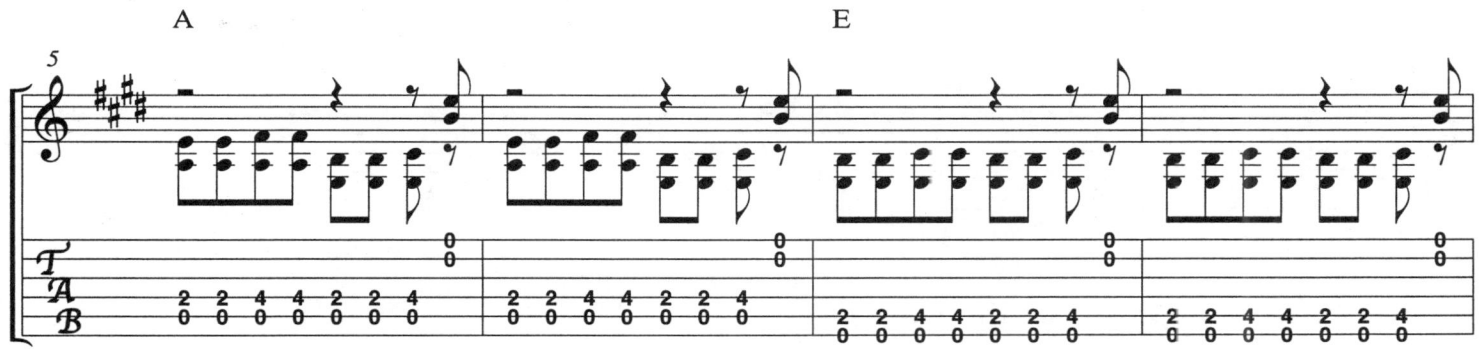
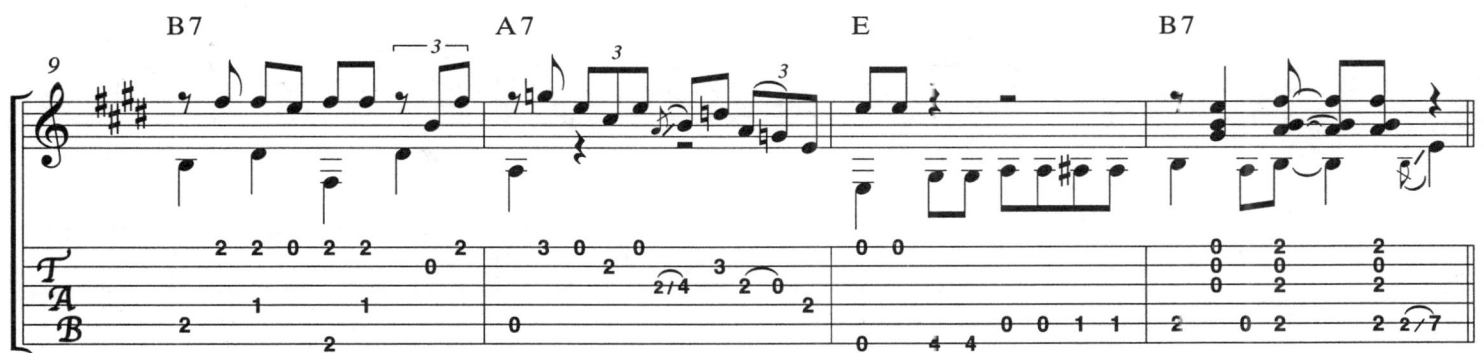
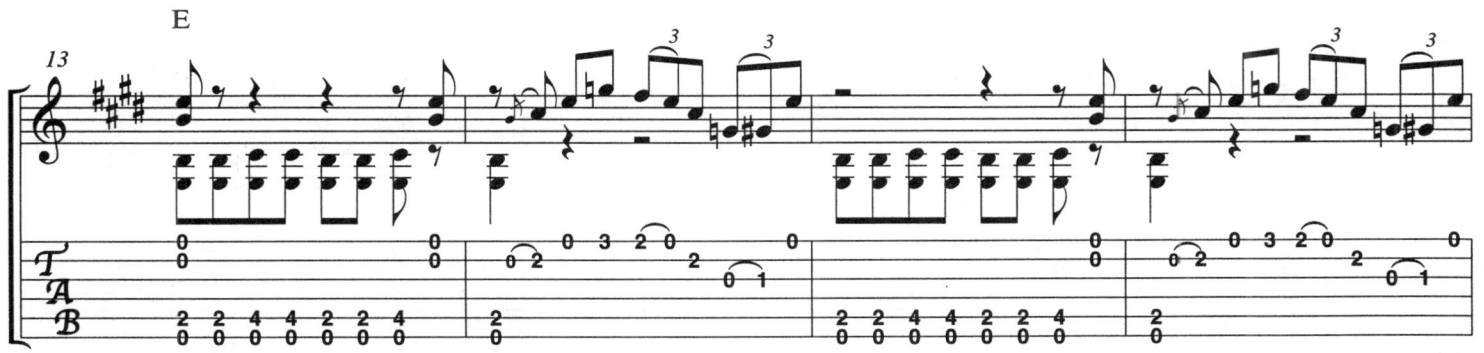

Lightnin' Strikes - 7 - 1
SAIR011

© 2002 Original Solid Air Records Music (BMI)
All Rights Reserved

50

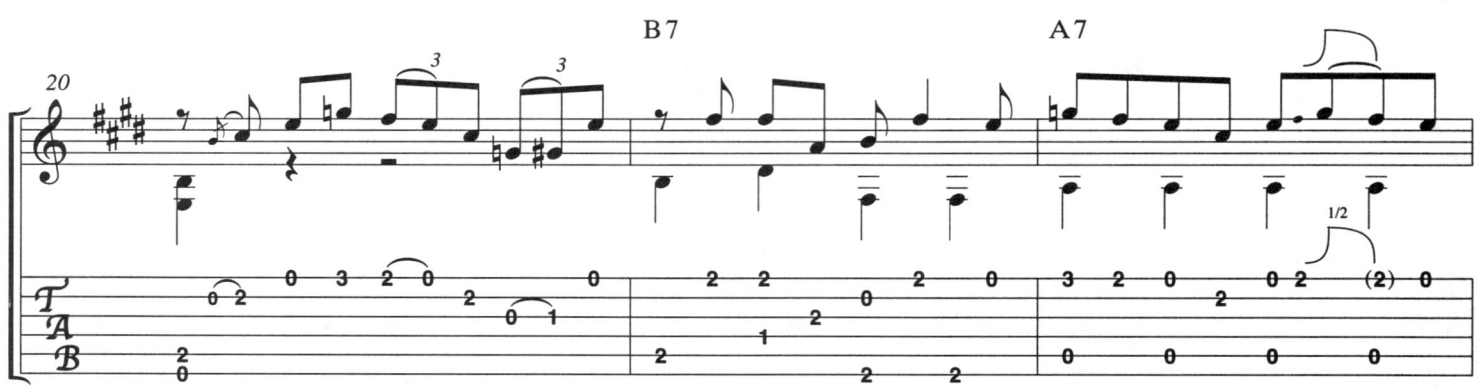
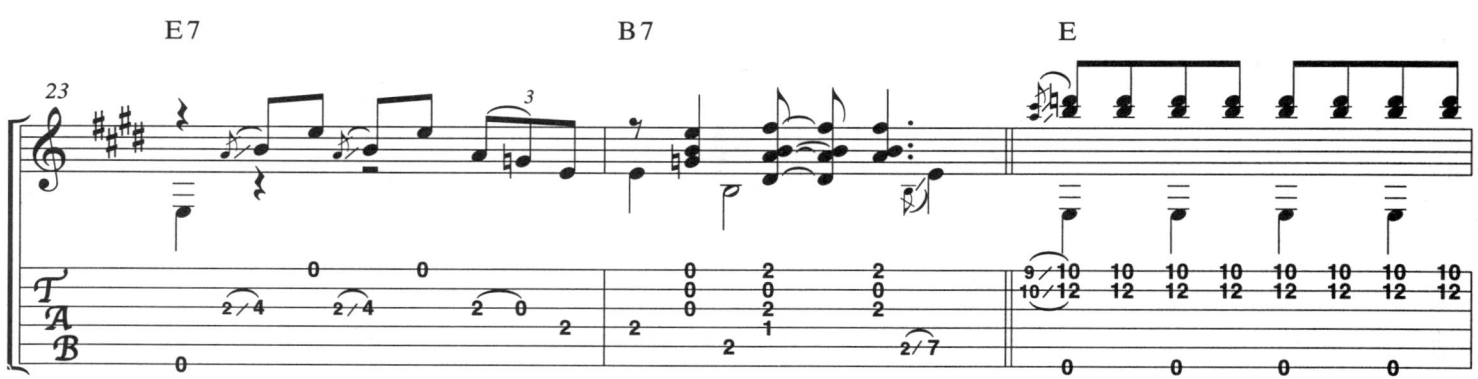
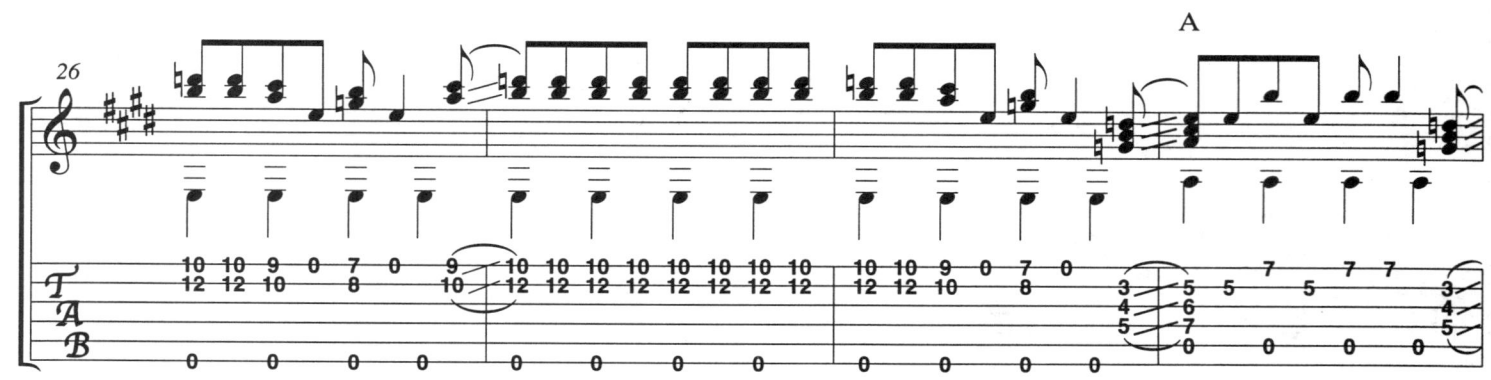

Lightnin' Strikes - 7 - 2
SAIR011

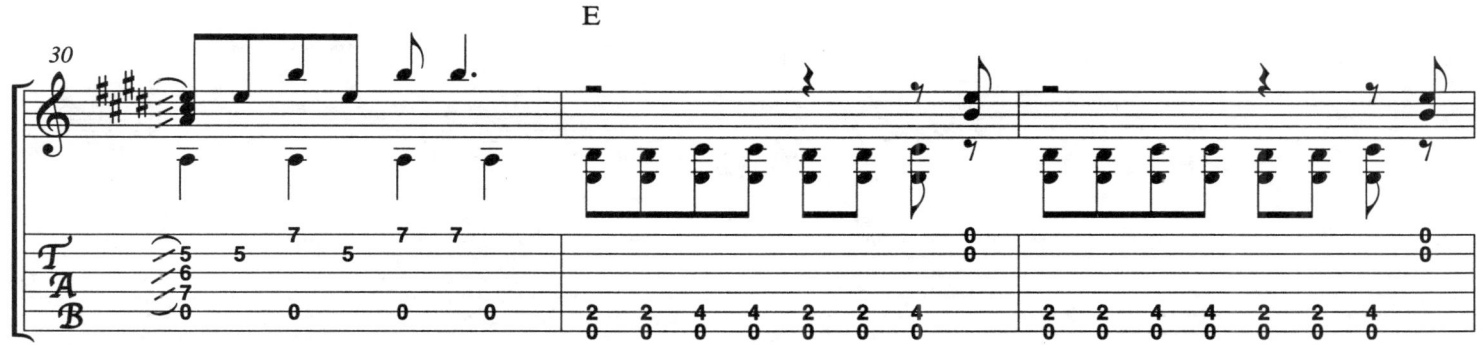
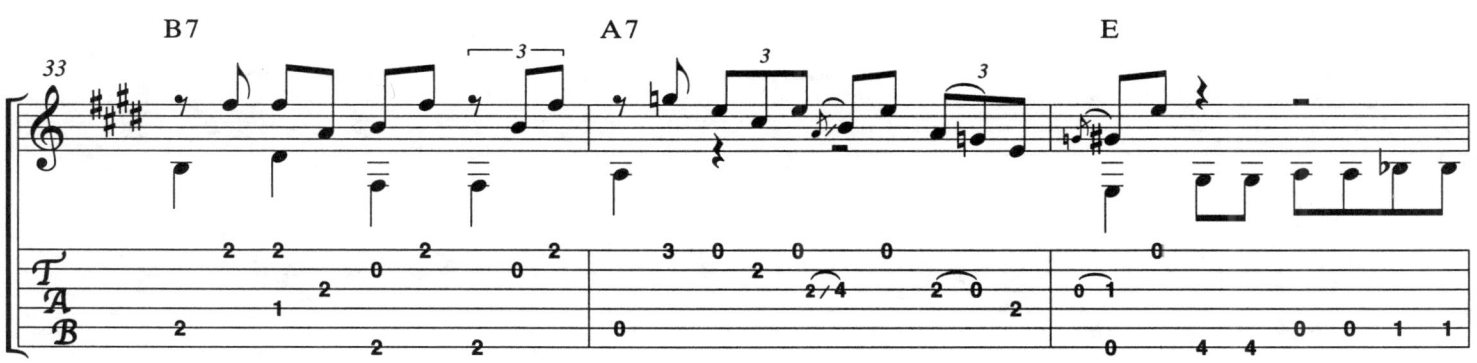
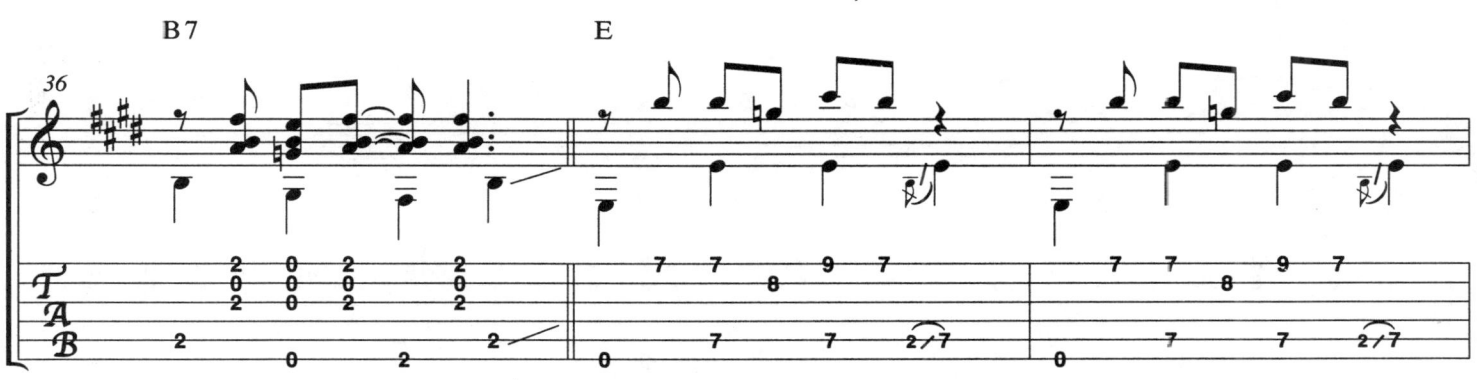
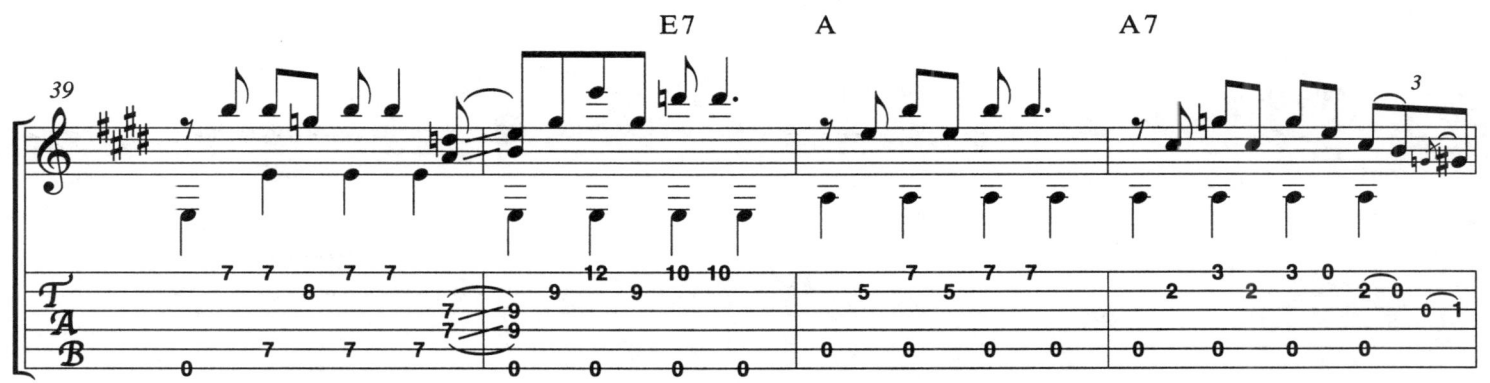

52

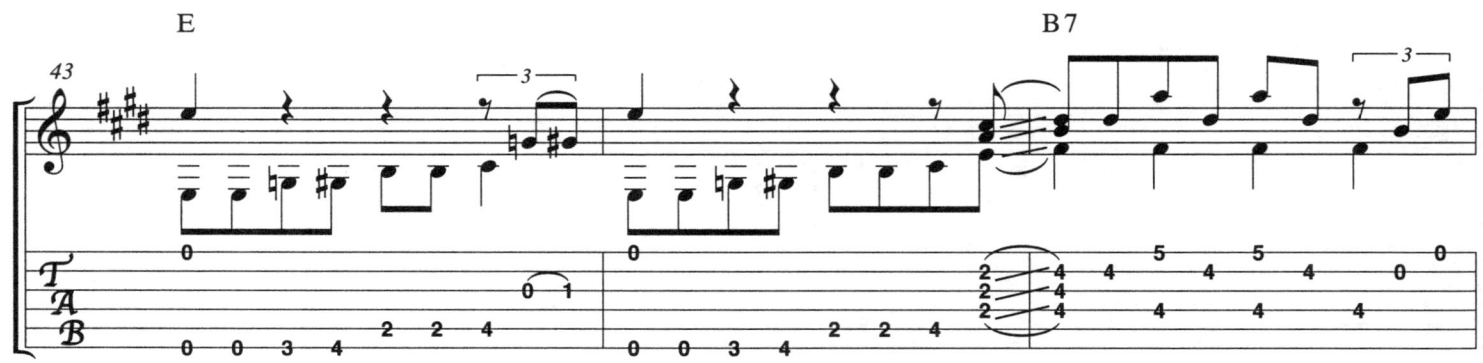
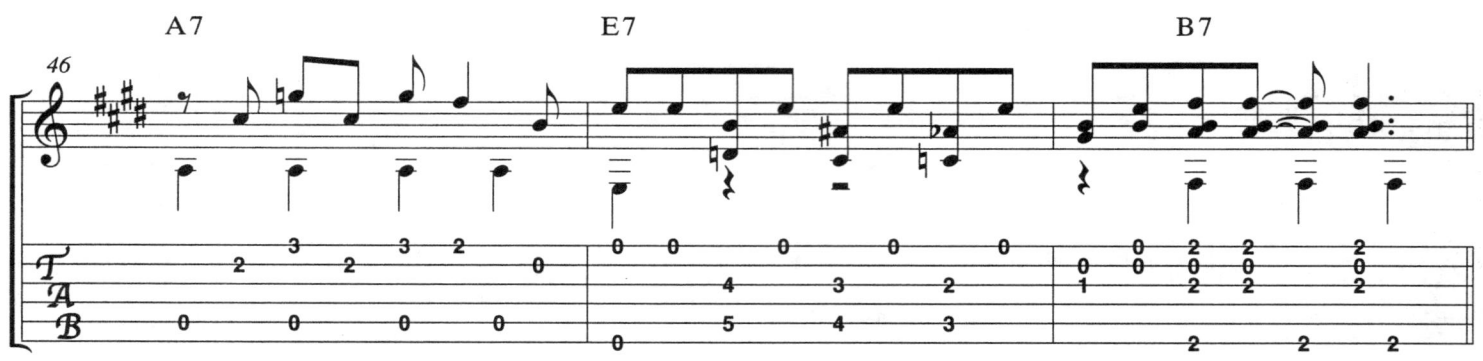
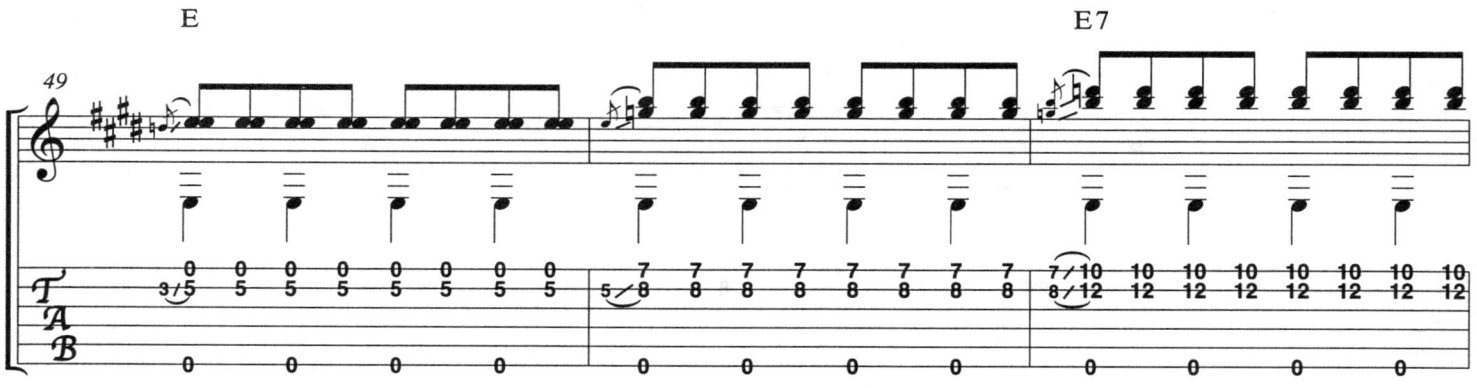
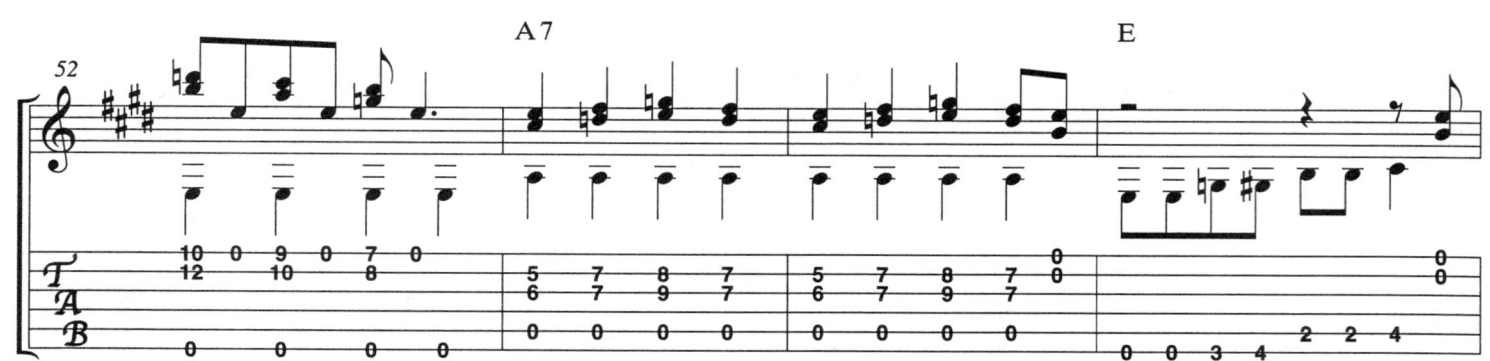

Lightnin' Strikes - 7 - 4
SAIR011

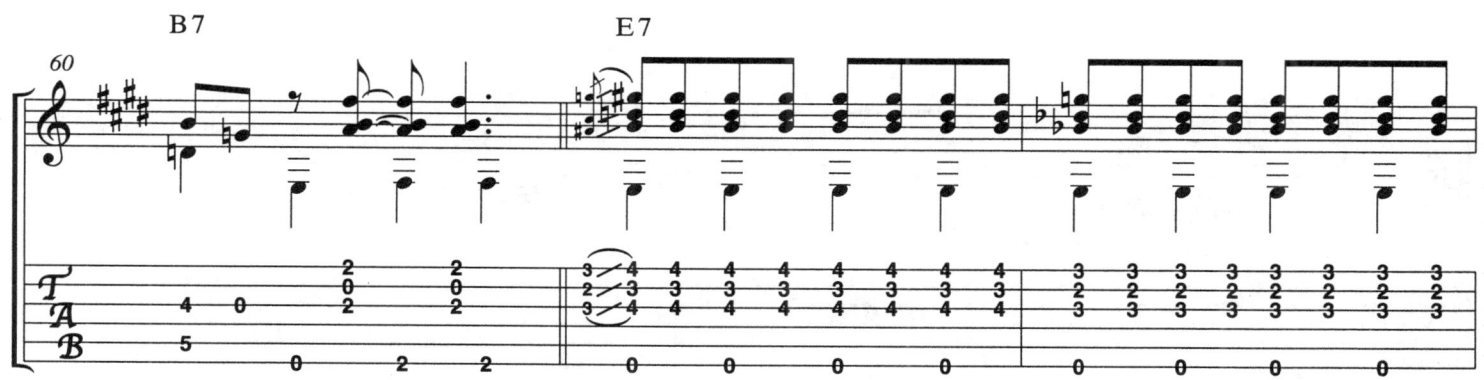
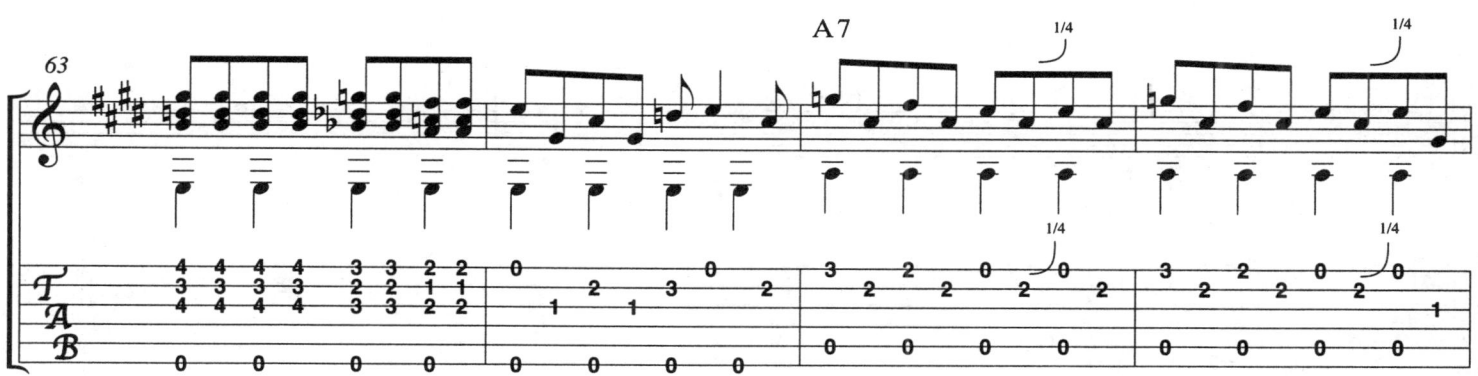
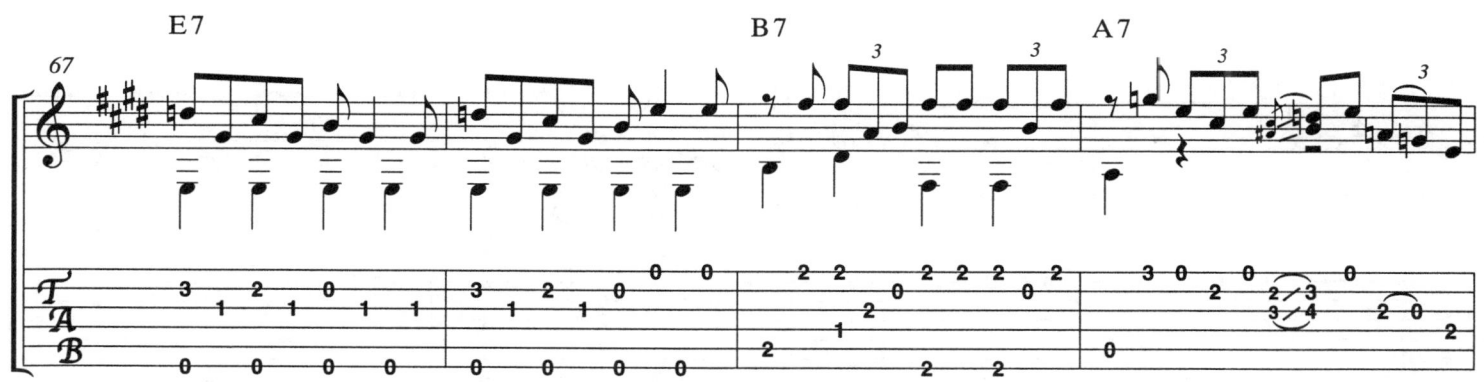

Lightnin' Strikes - 7 - 5
SAIR011

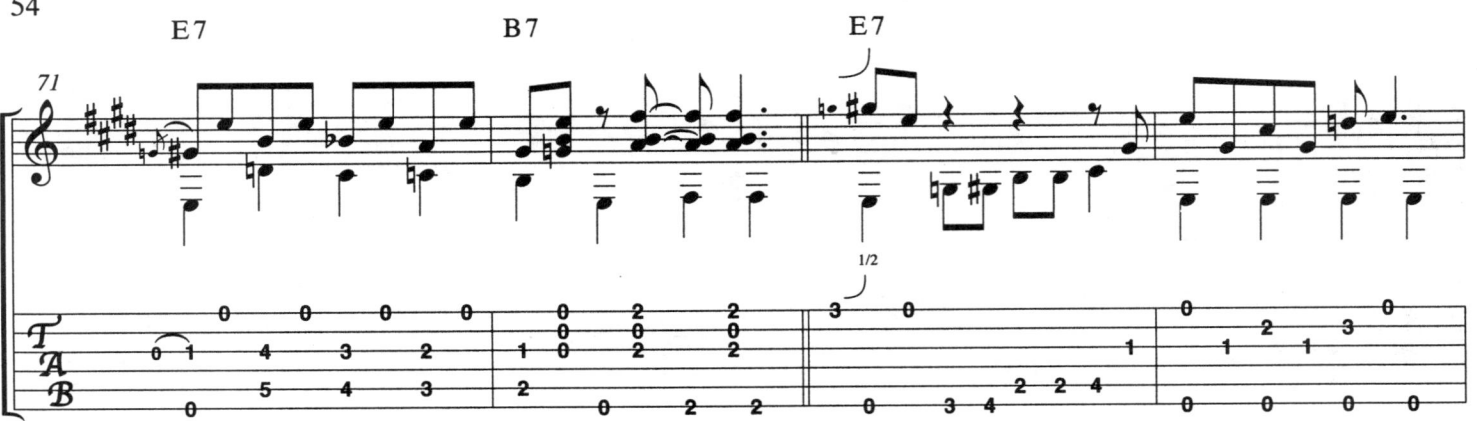
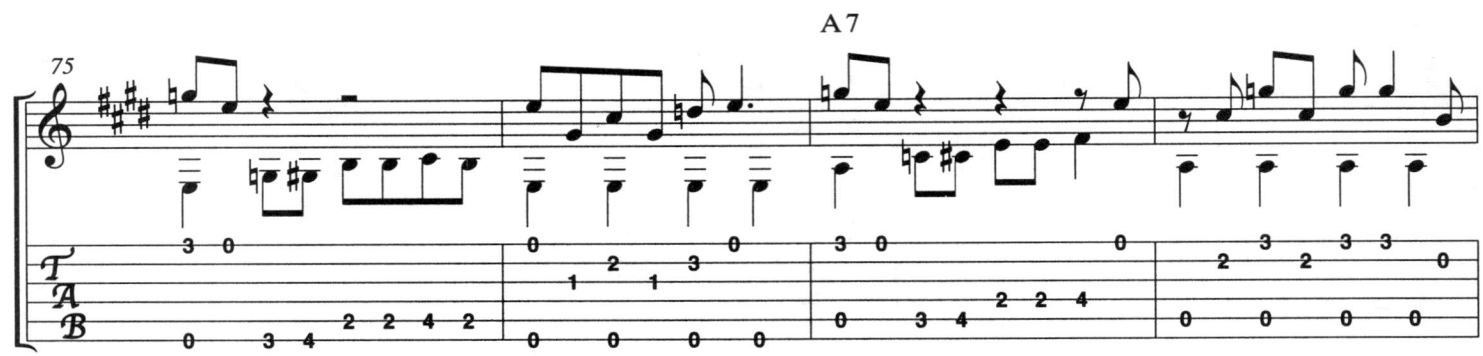
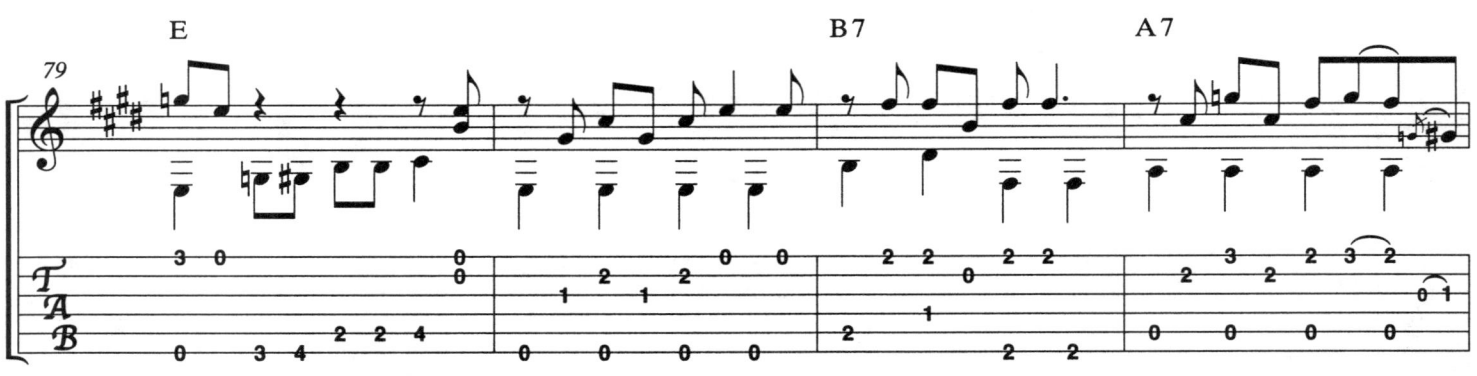
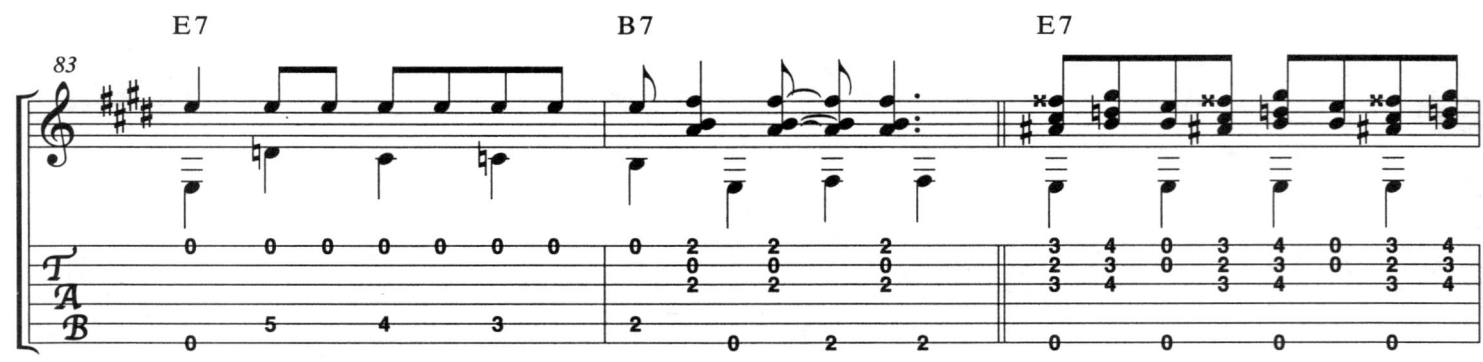

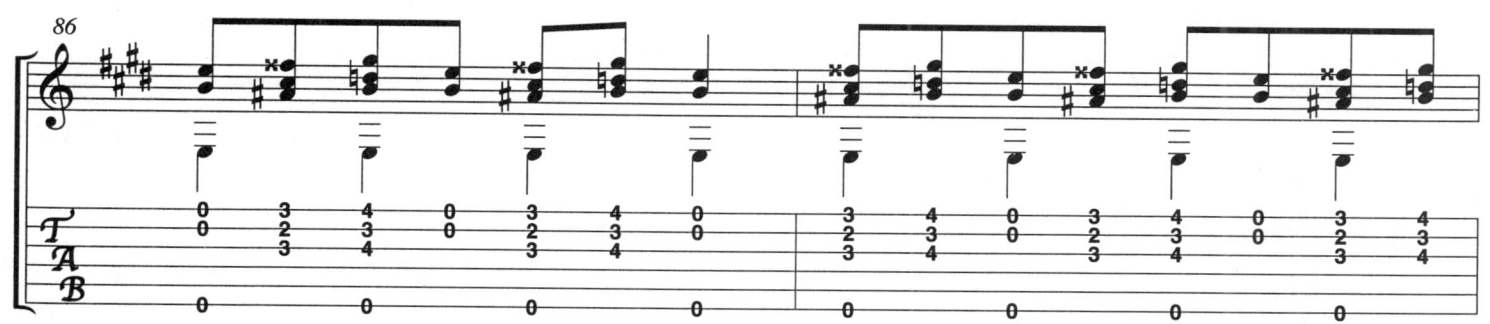
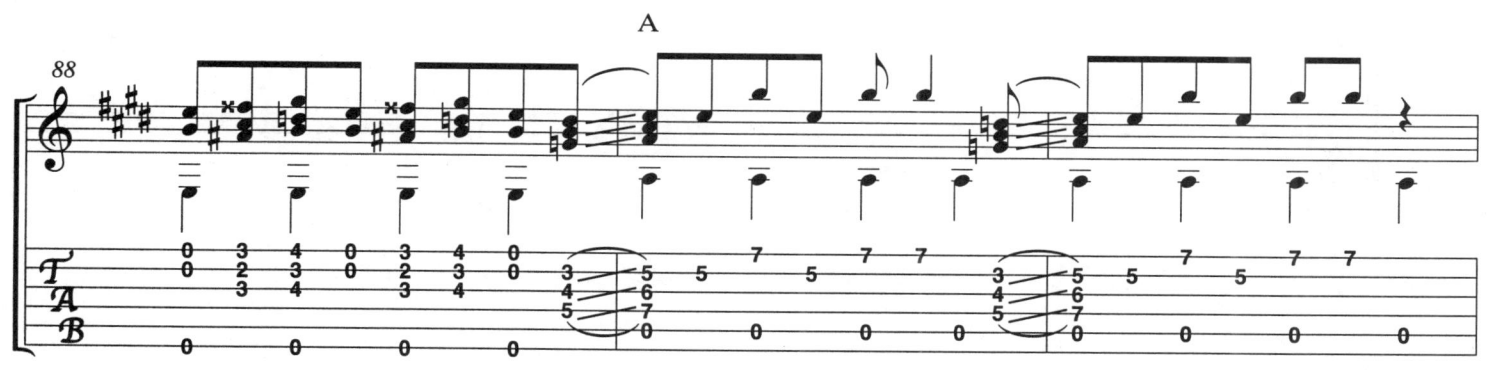

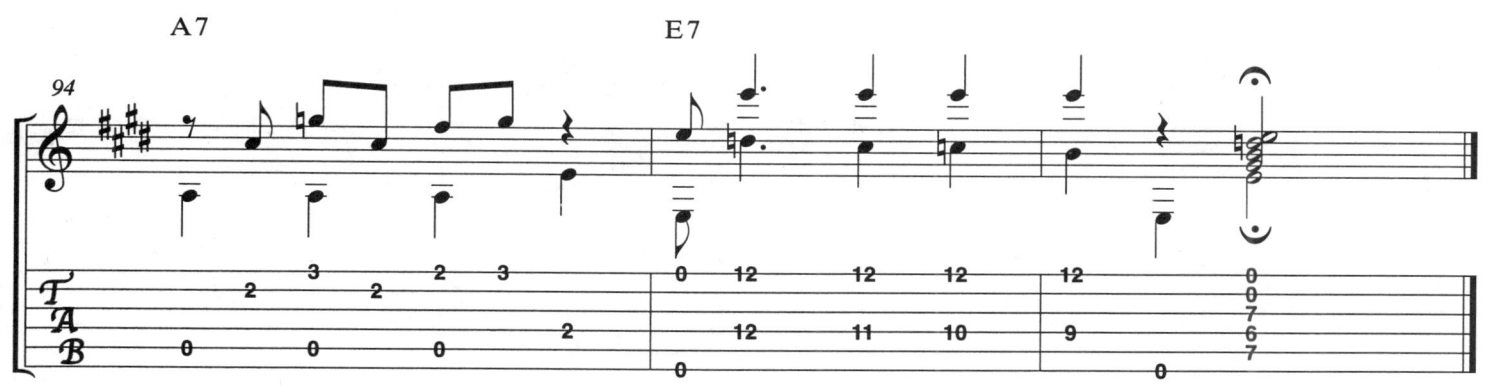

Meant To Be

By AL PETTEWAY

Tune to DADGAD:
⑥ = D   ③ = G
⑤ = A   ②= A
④ = D   ① = D

Moderately ♩ = 105

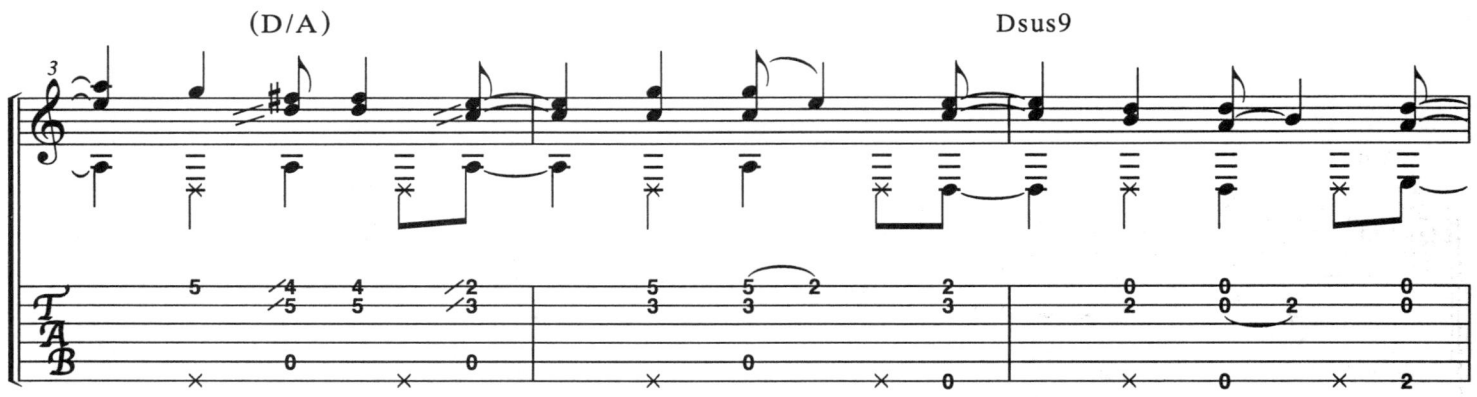

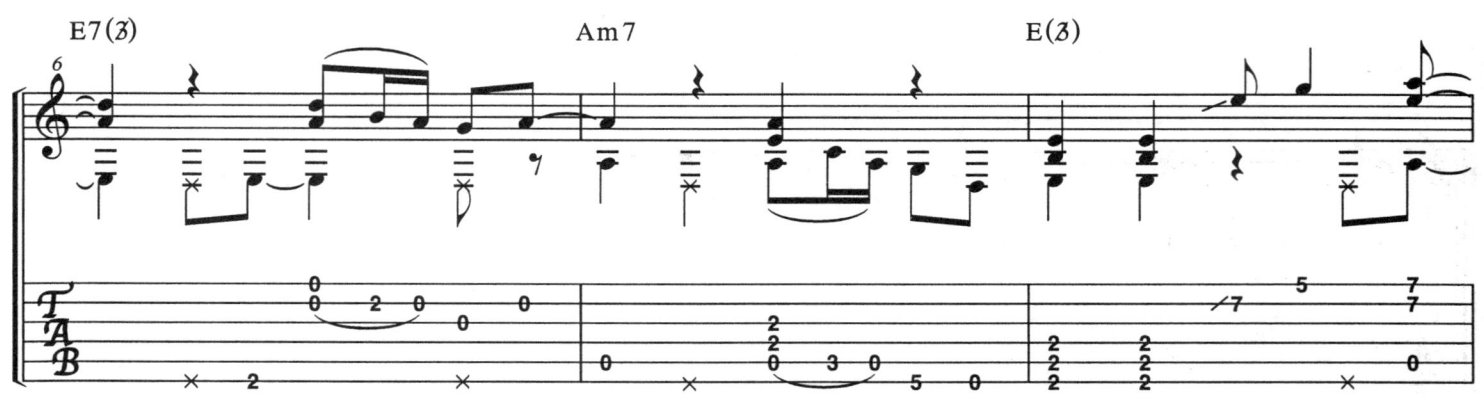

Meant to Be - 5 - 1
SAIR011

© 2002 Al Petteway (BMI)
All Rights Reserved

58

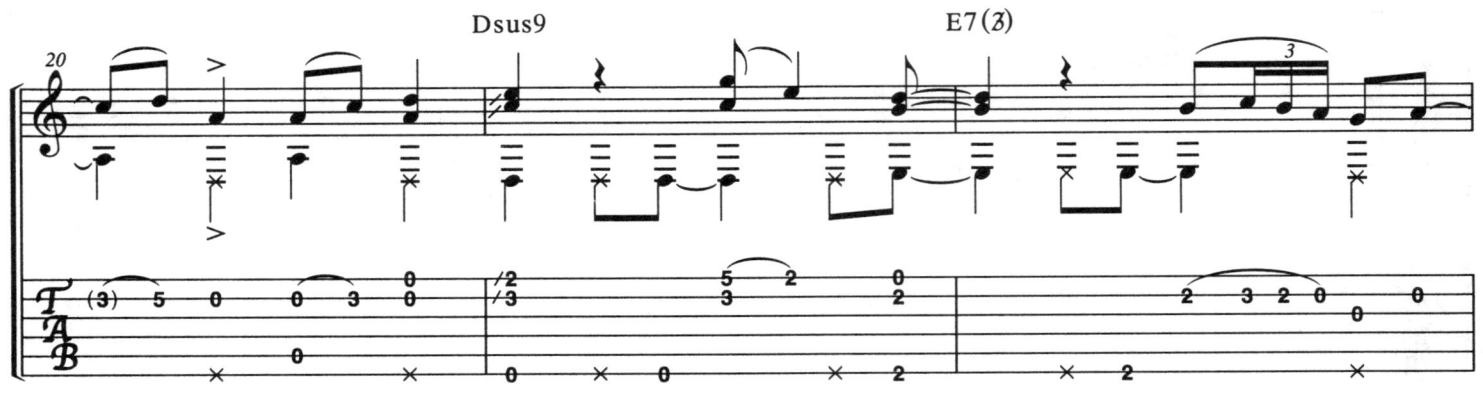

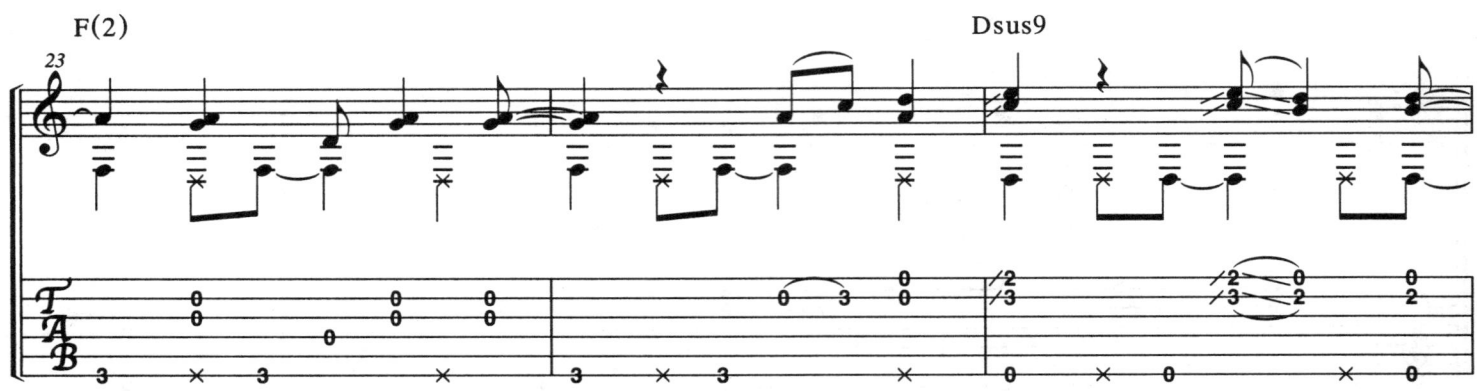

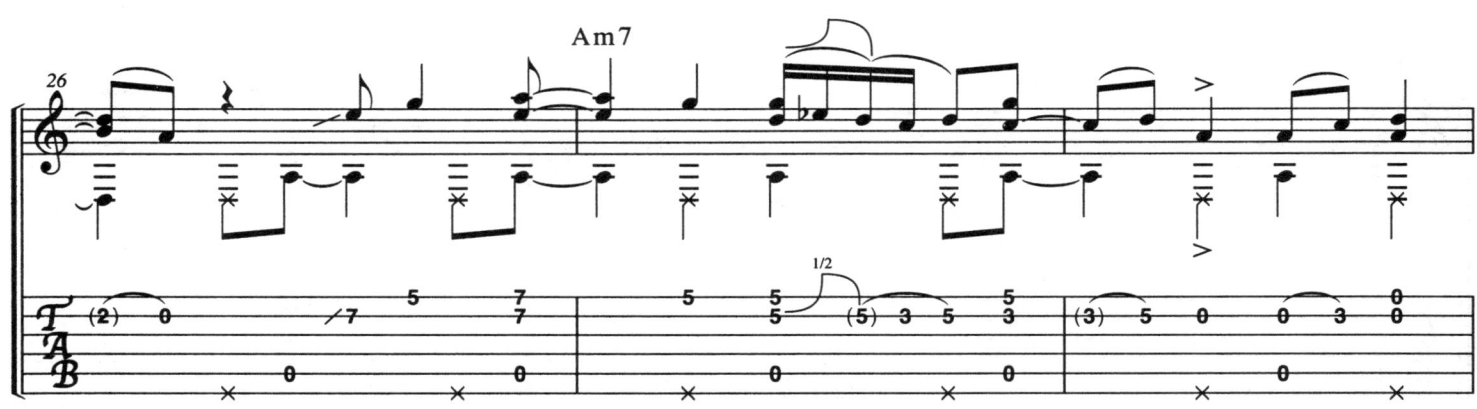

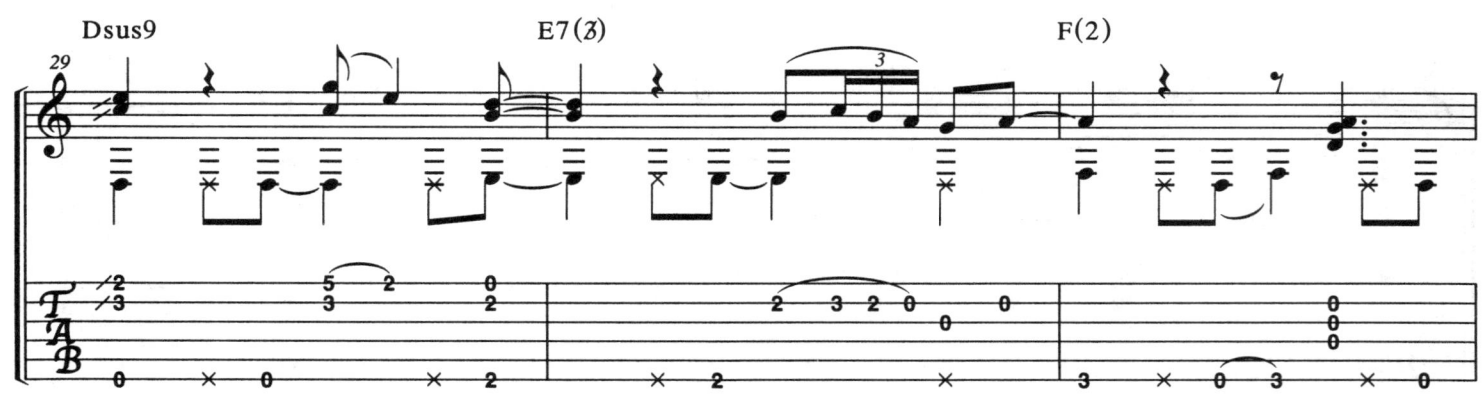

Meant to Be - 5 - 3
SAIR011

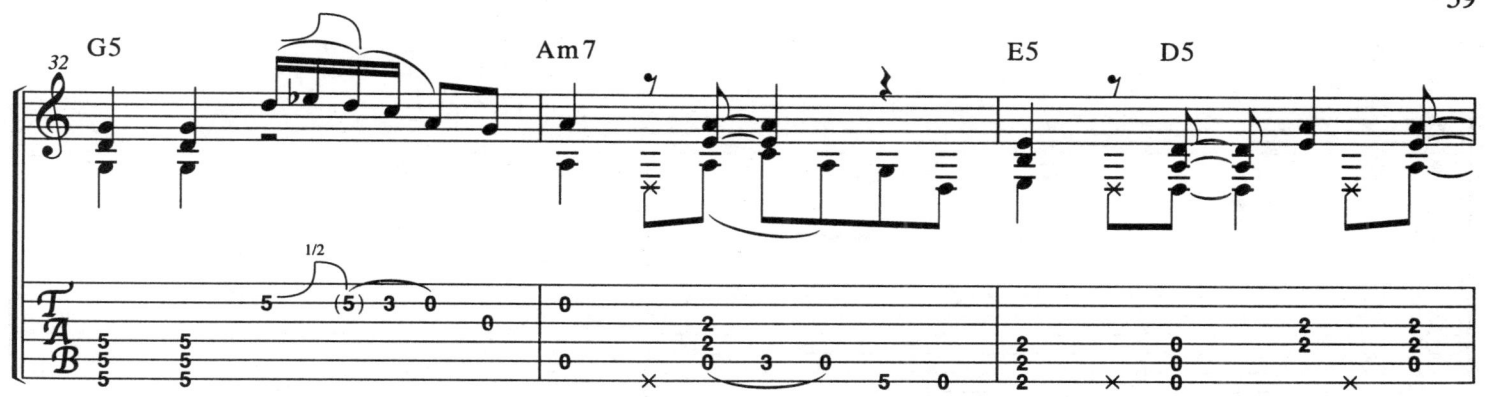
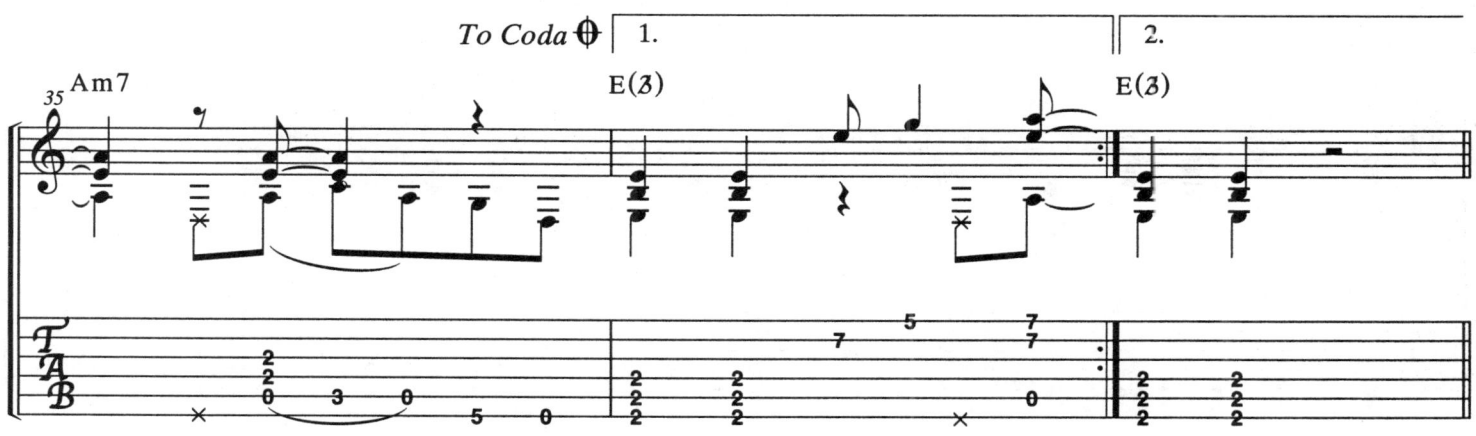
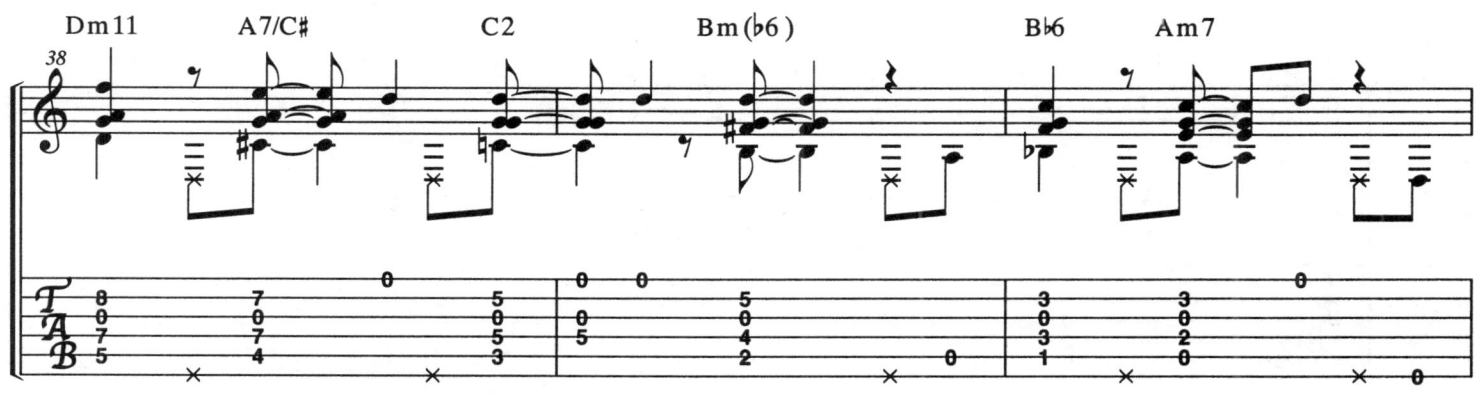
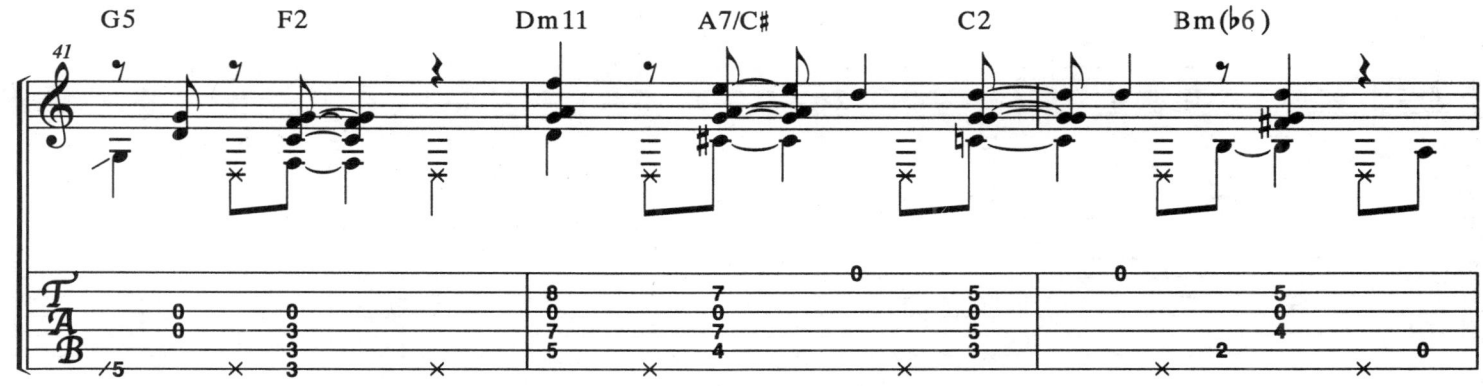

Meant to Be - 5 - 4
SAIR011

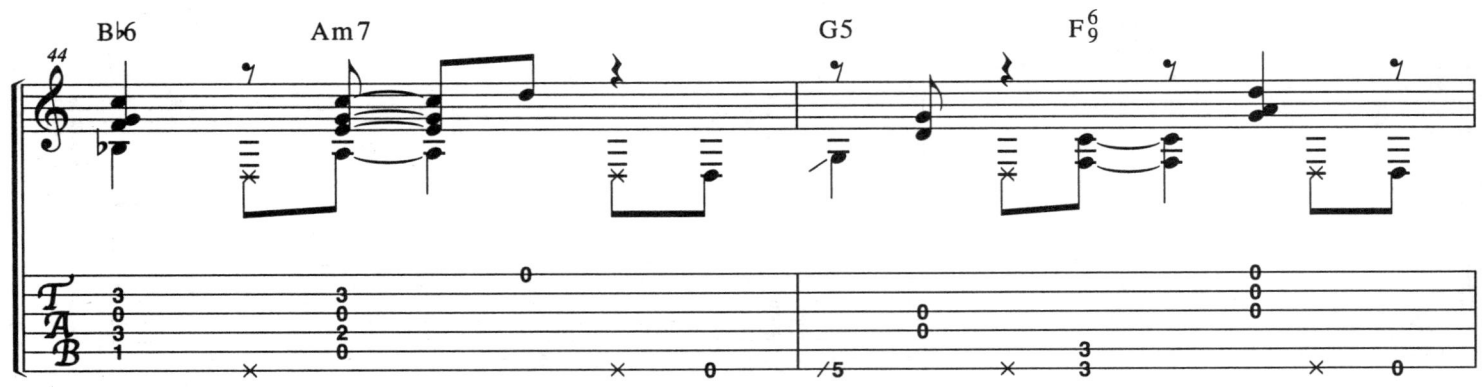
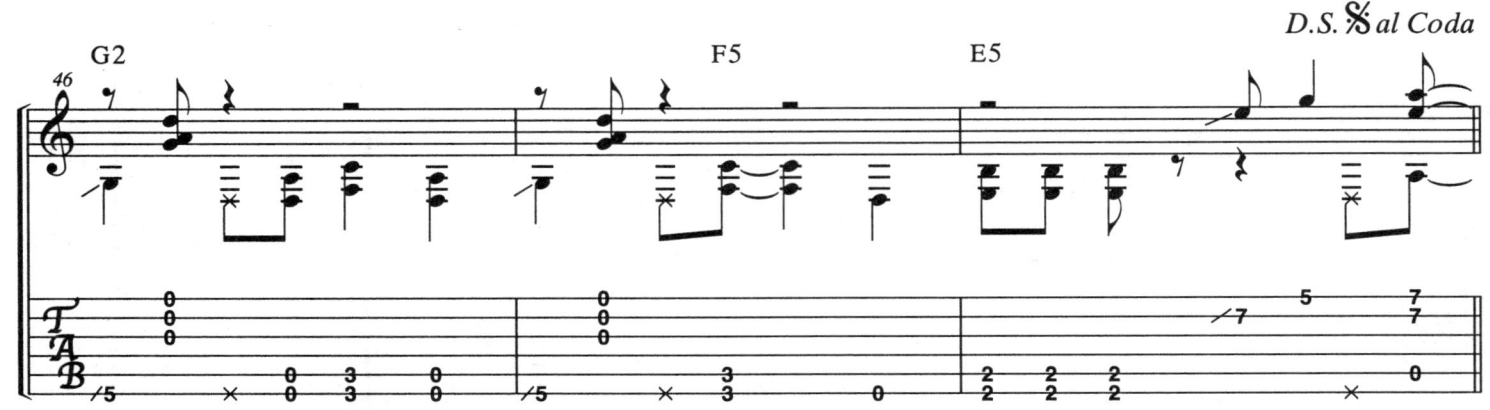
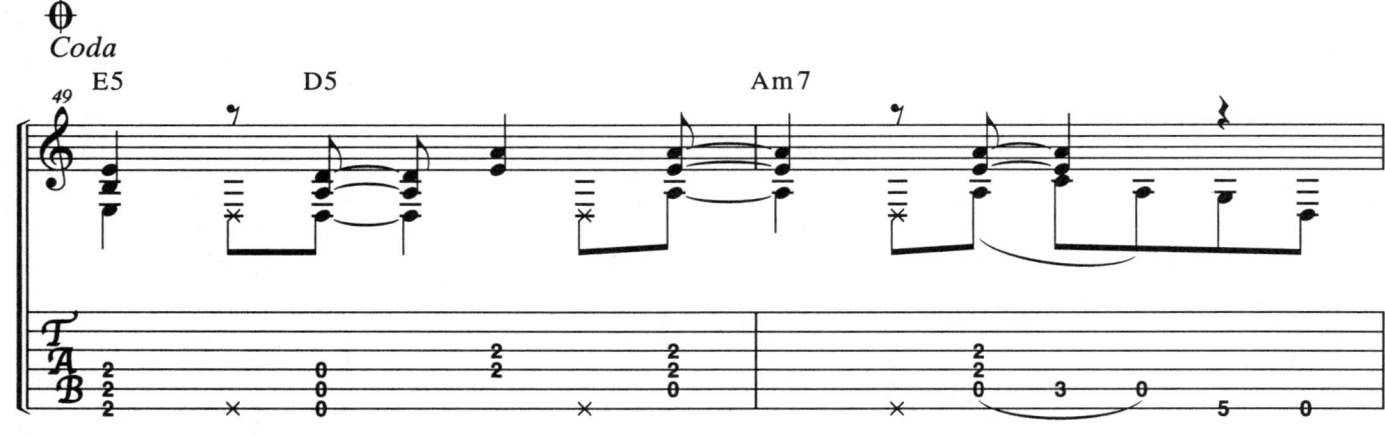
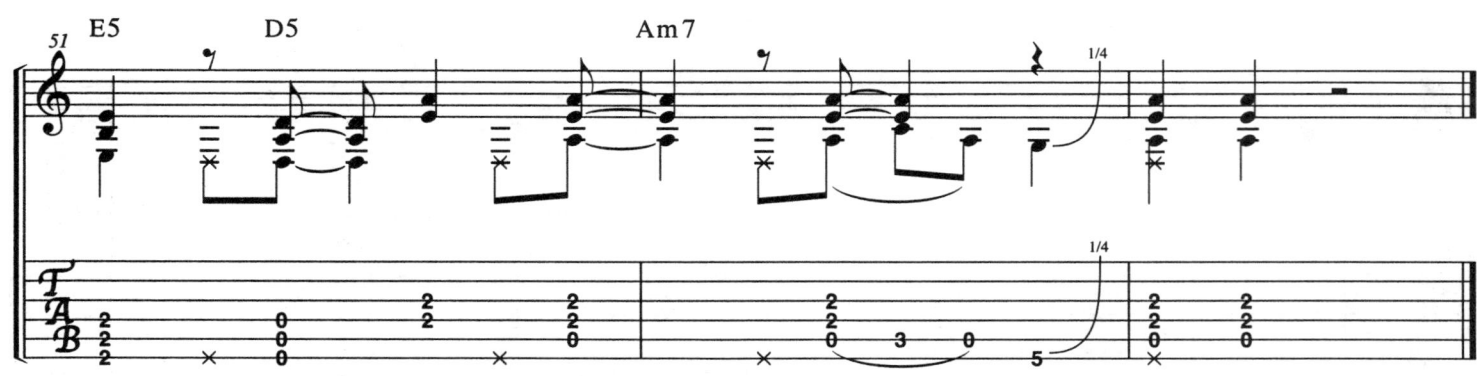

Minor Thing

By MIKE DOWLING and RANDY SABIEN

Minor Thing - 9 - 1
SAIR011

© 1995 TableTop Music (ASCAP) and Fiddlehead Music (BMI)
All Rights Reserved

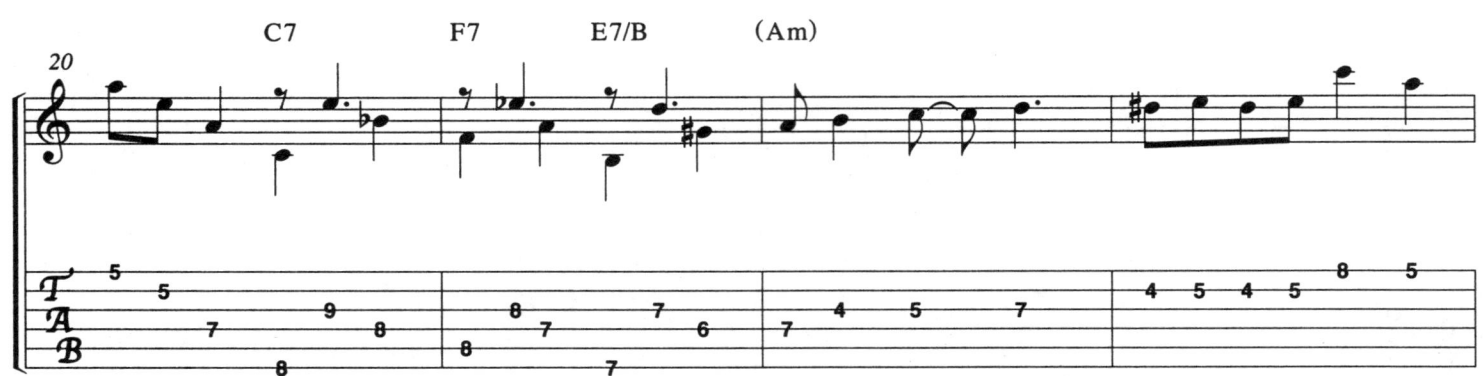
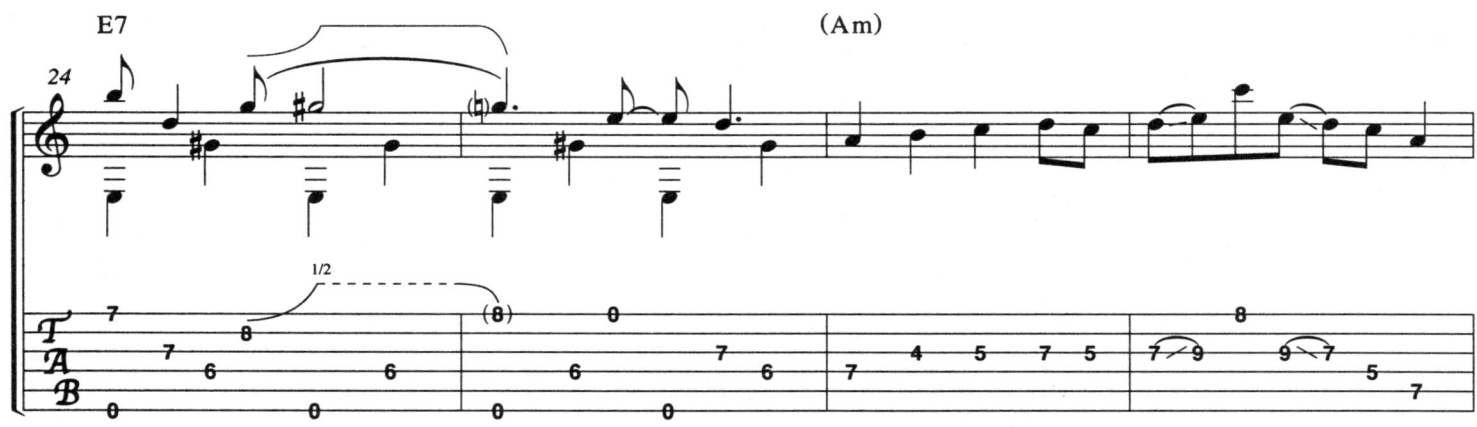
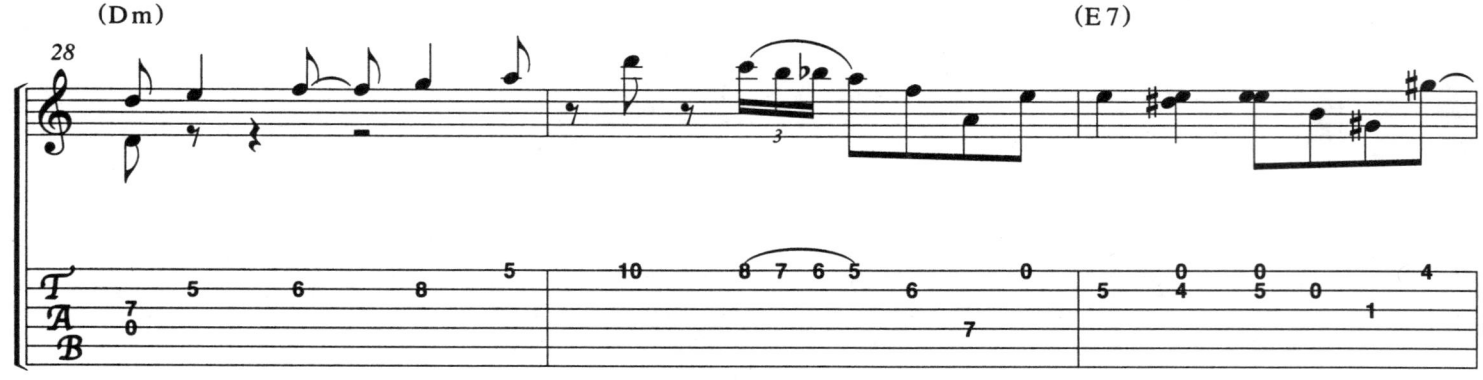

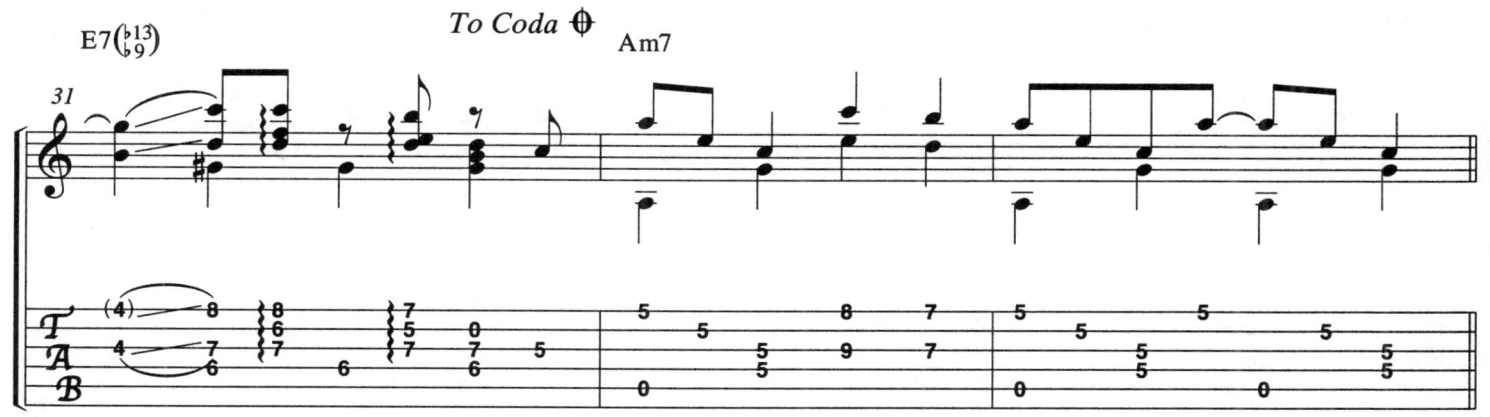
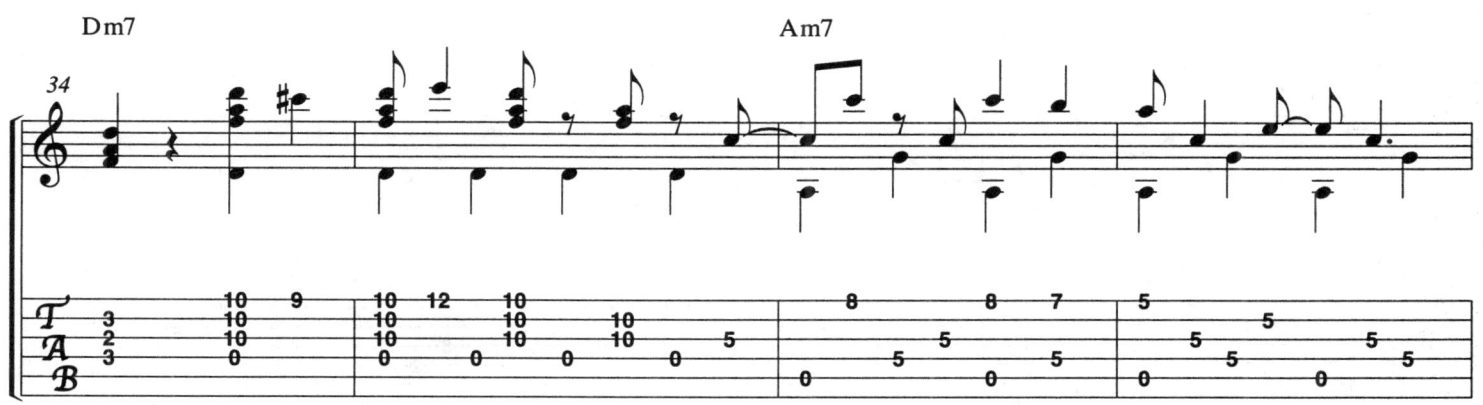
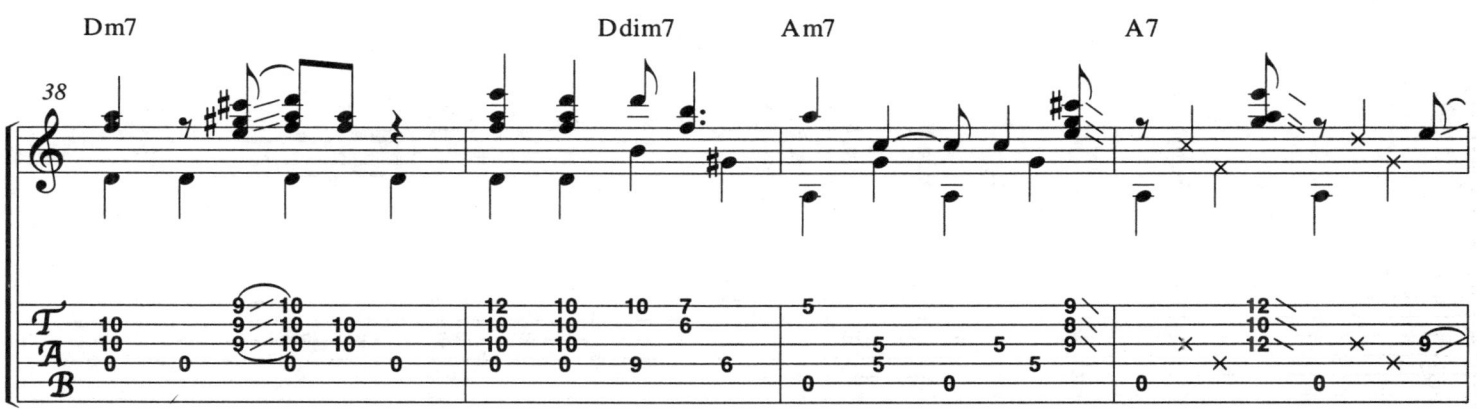
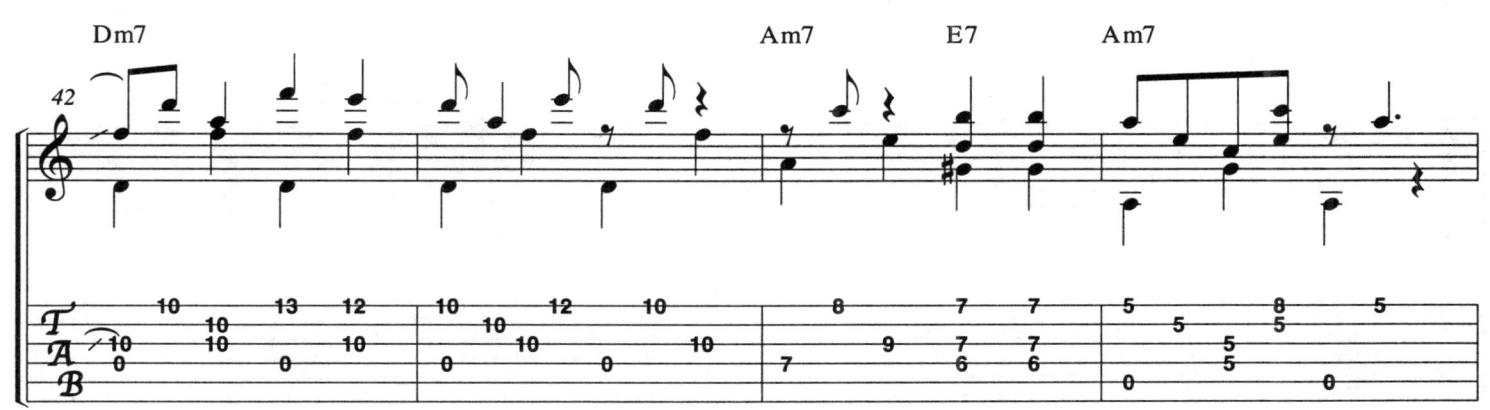

Minor Thing - 9 - 3
SAIR011

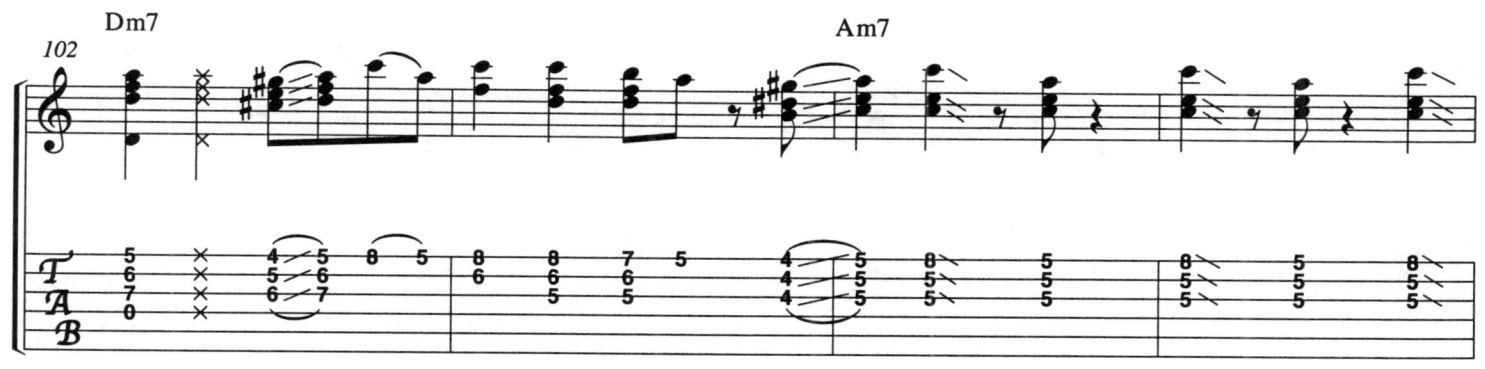

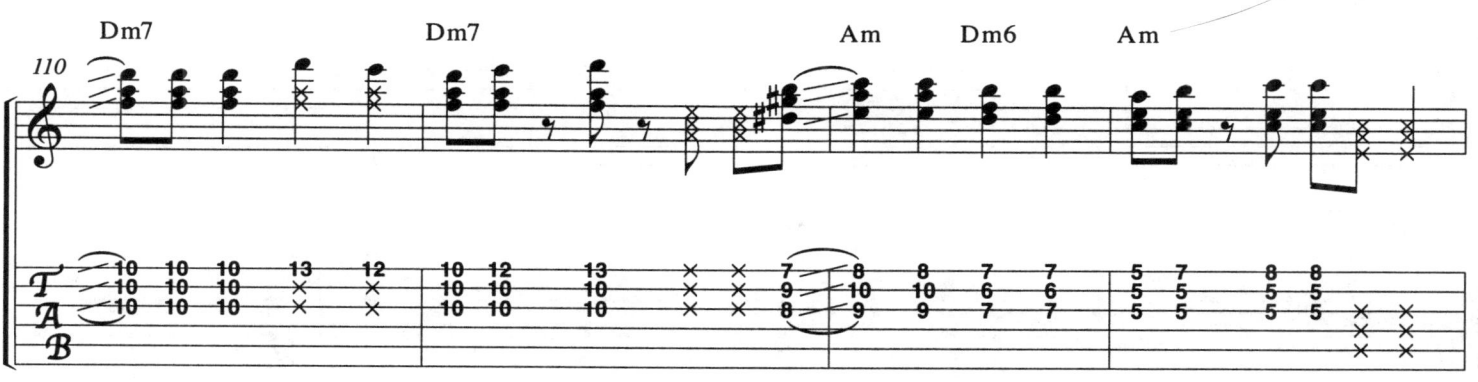
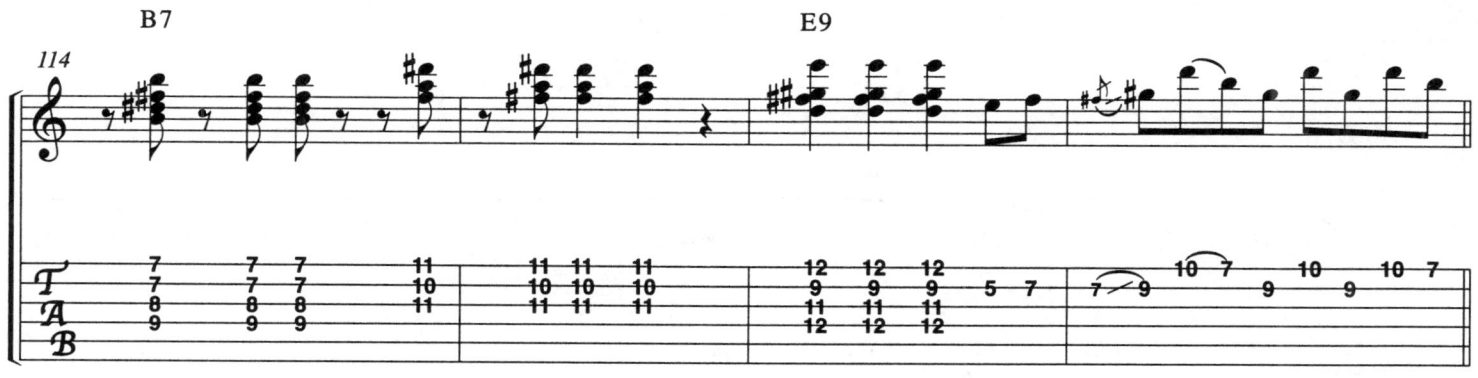

68

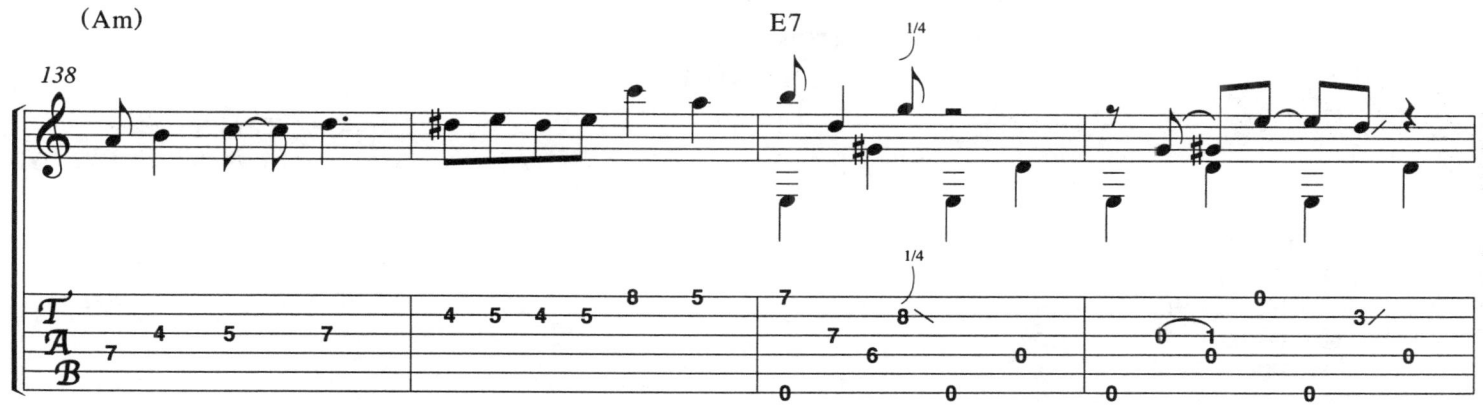

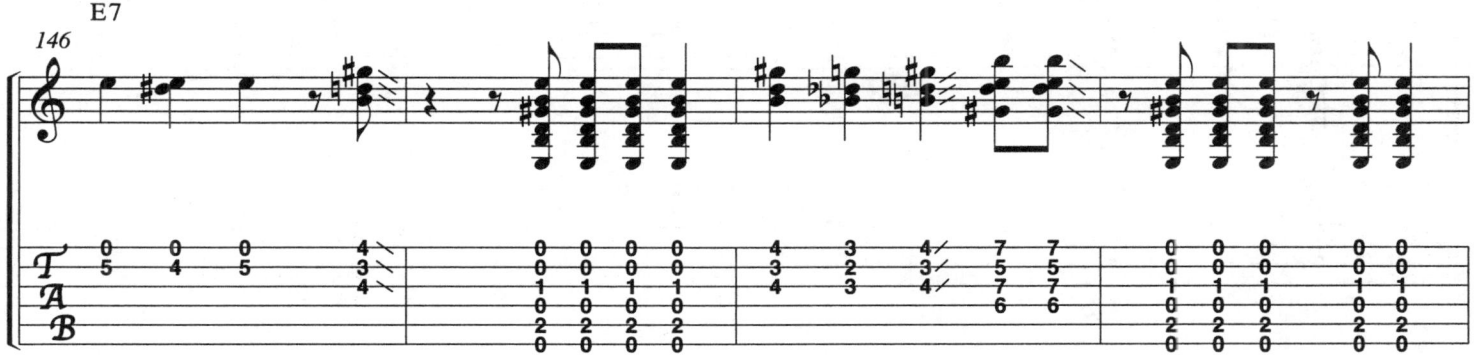
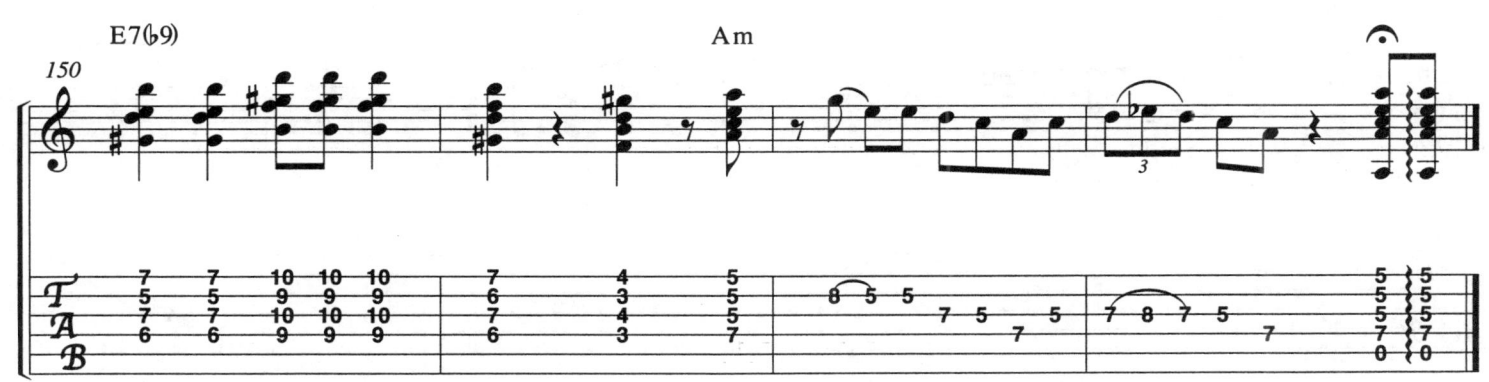

Rosalie

Traditional
Arranged by MIKE DOWLING

Open G tuning:
⑥ = D   ③ = G
⑤ = G   ② = B
④ = D   ① = D

*Brush with back of right-hand fingernails to produce a percussive backbeat.

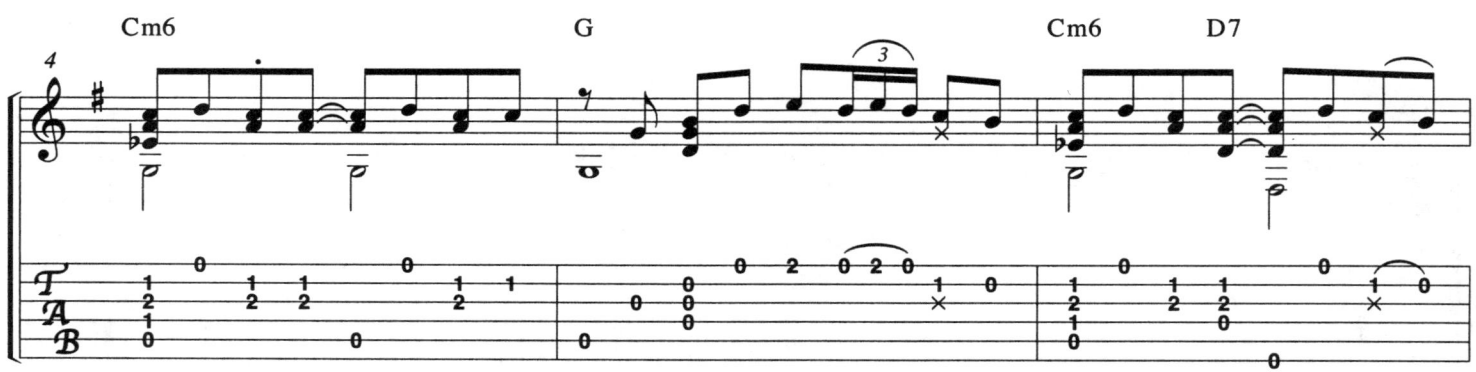

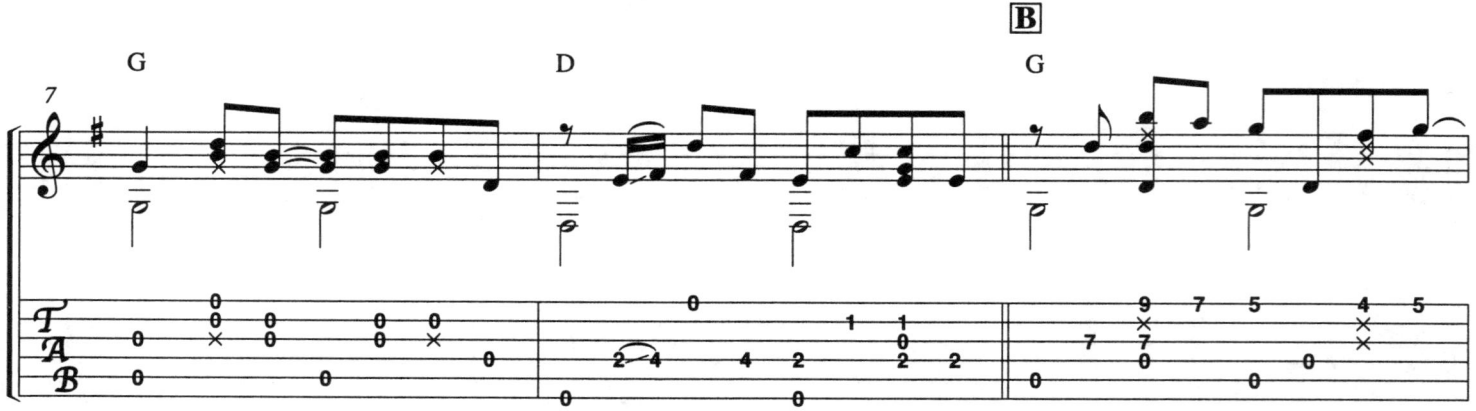

Rosalie - 6 - 1
SAIR011

© 1995 TableTop Music (ASCAP) and Solid Air Music (ASCAP)
All Rights Reserved

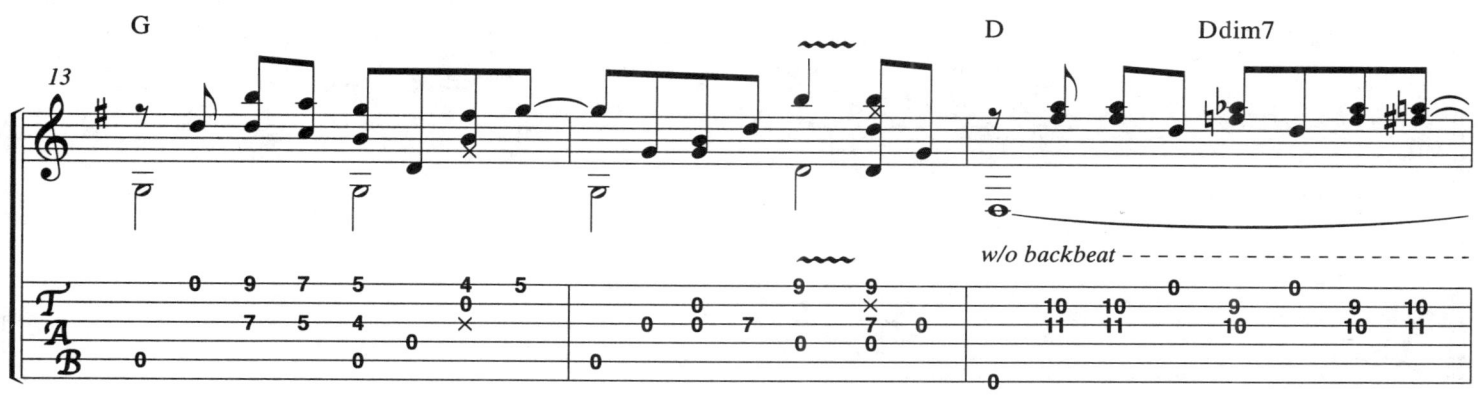

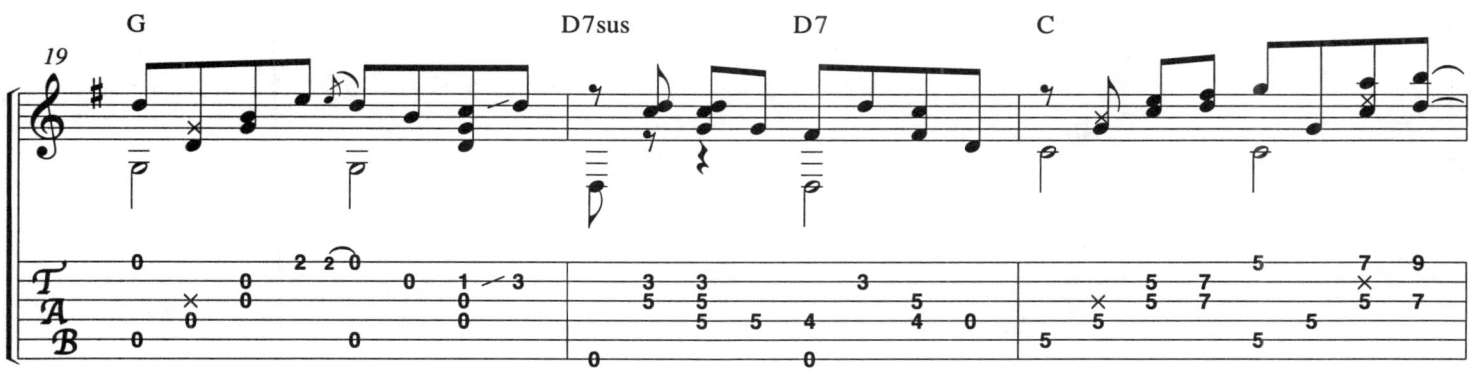

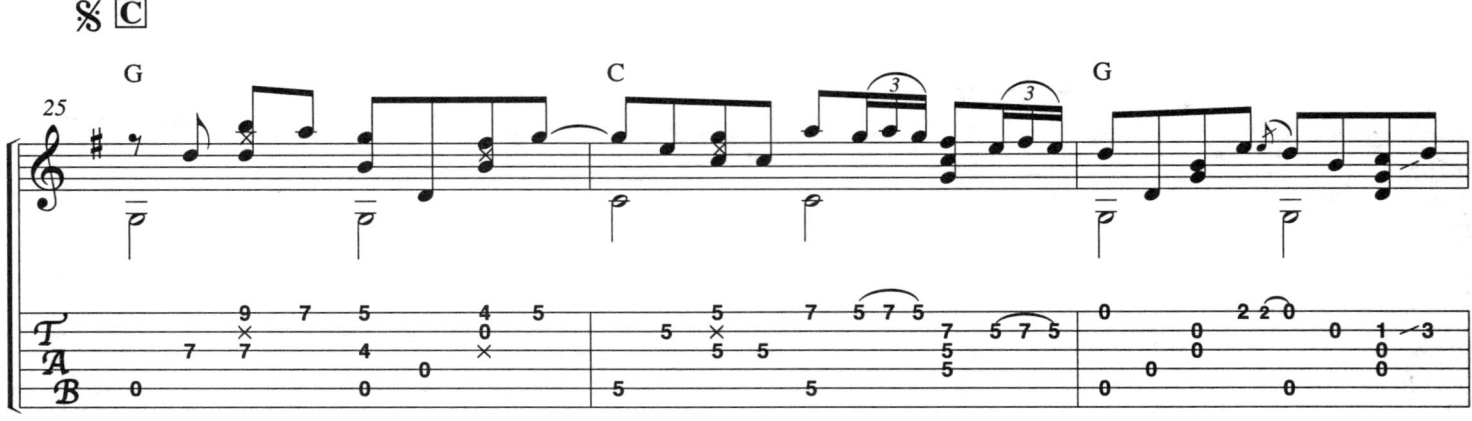
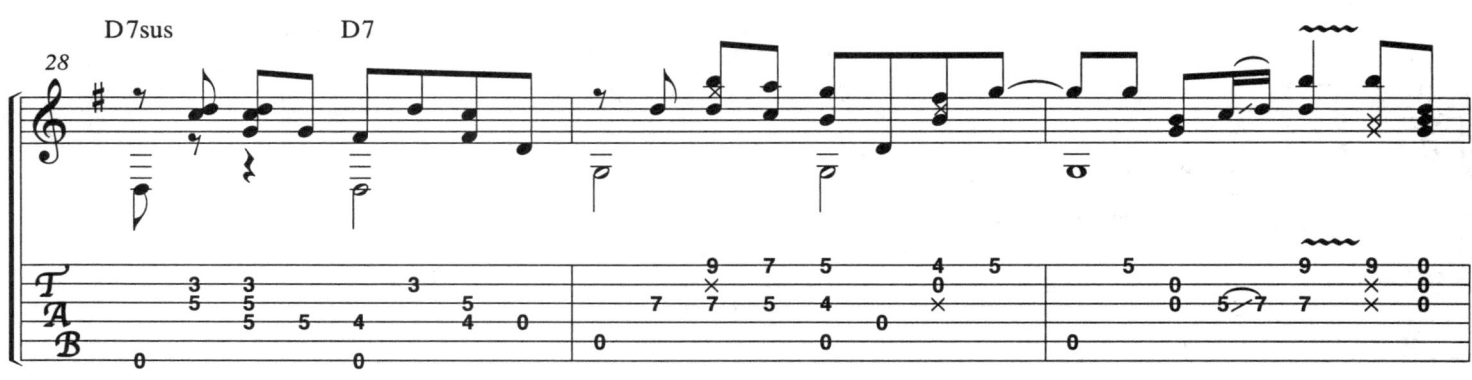
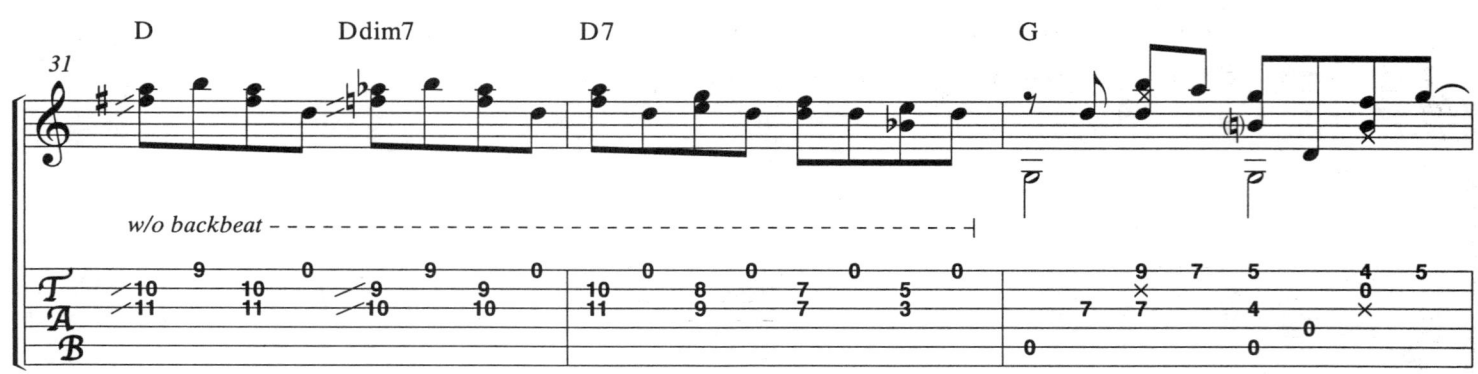

73

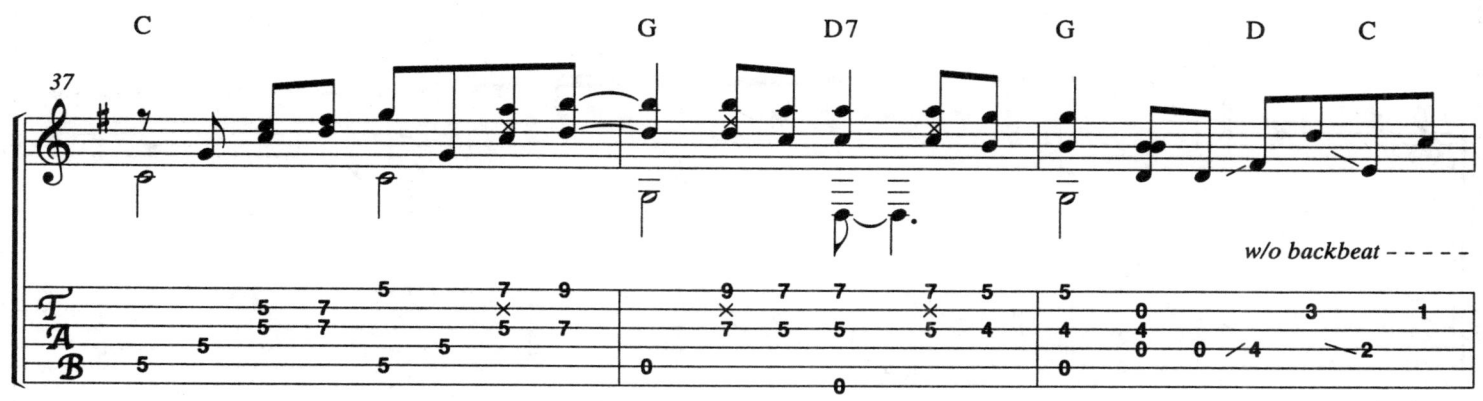
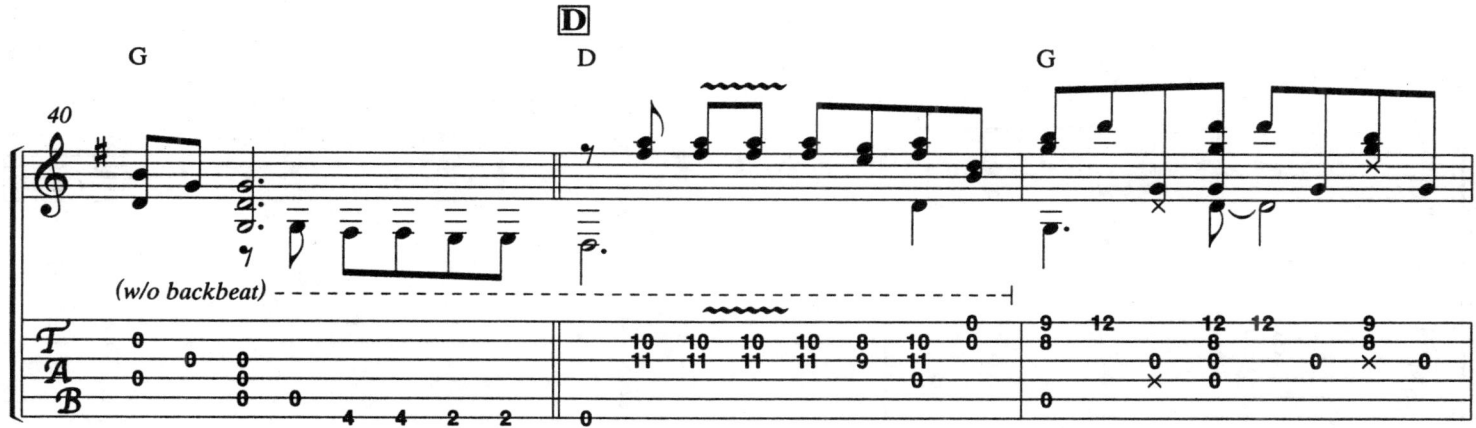
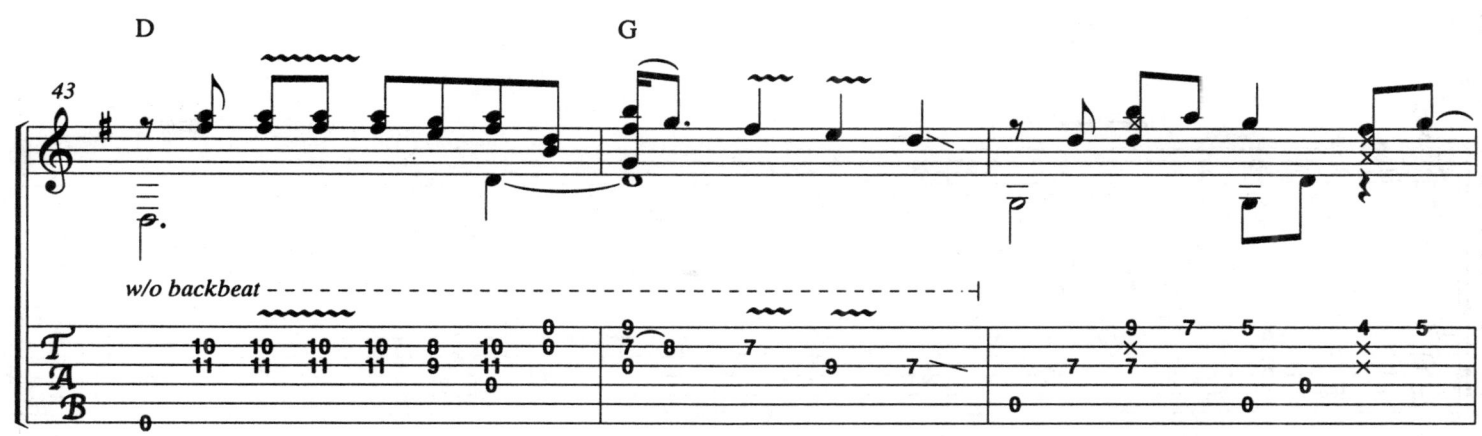

Rosalie - 6 - 4
SAIR011

74

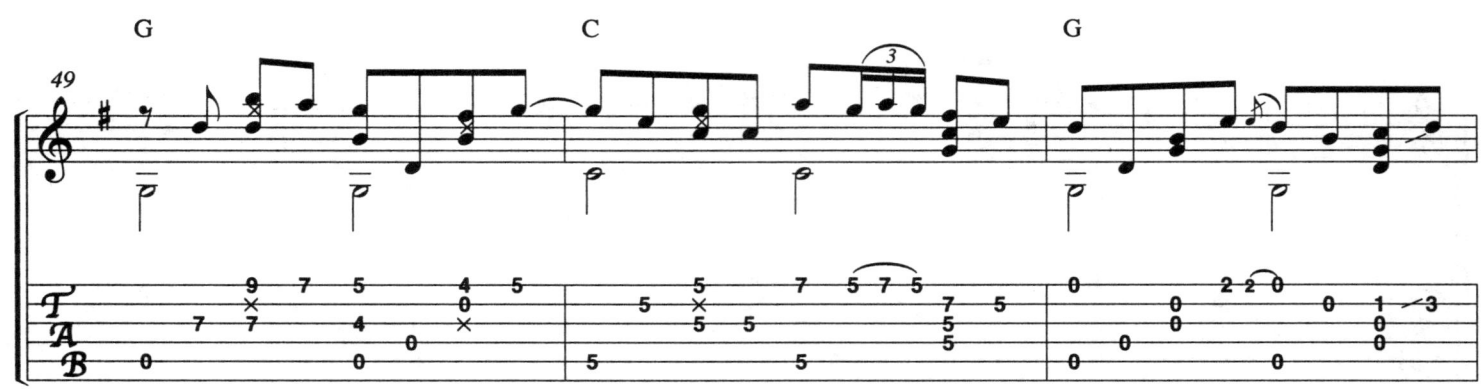
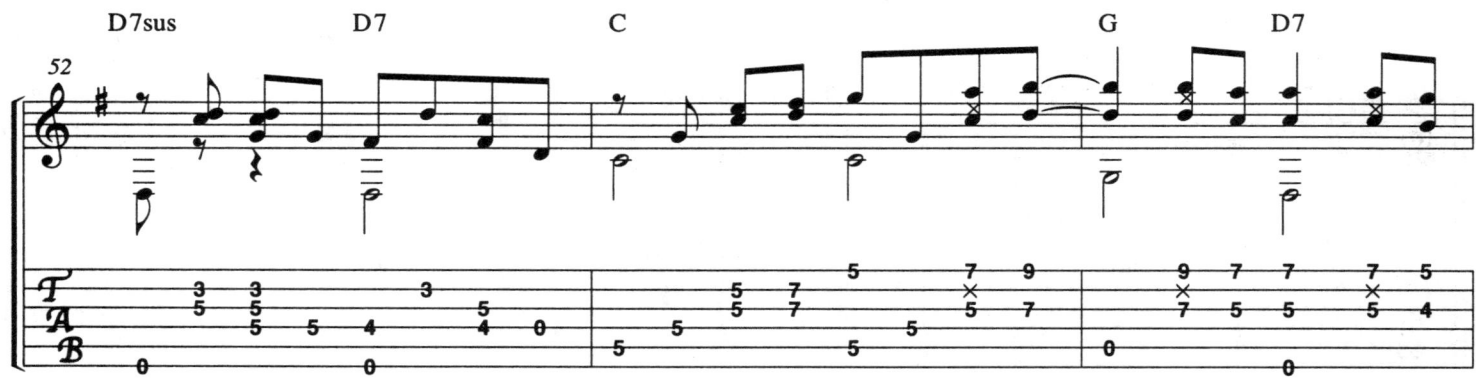
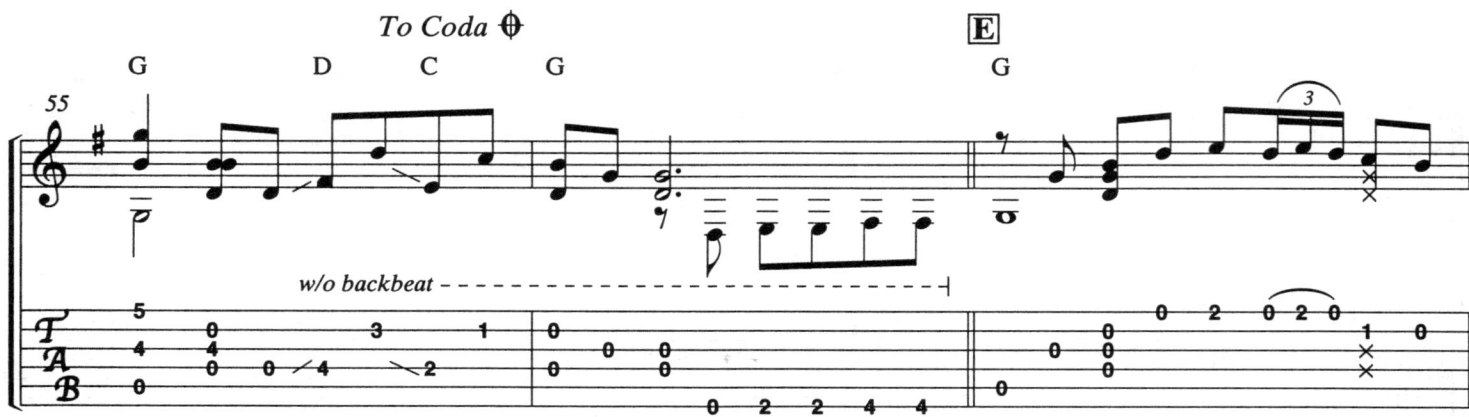

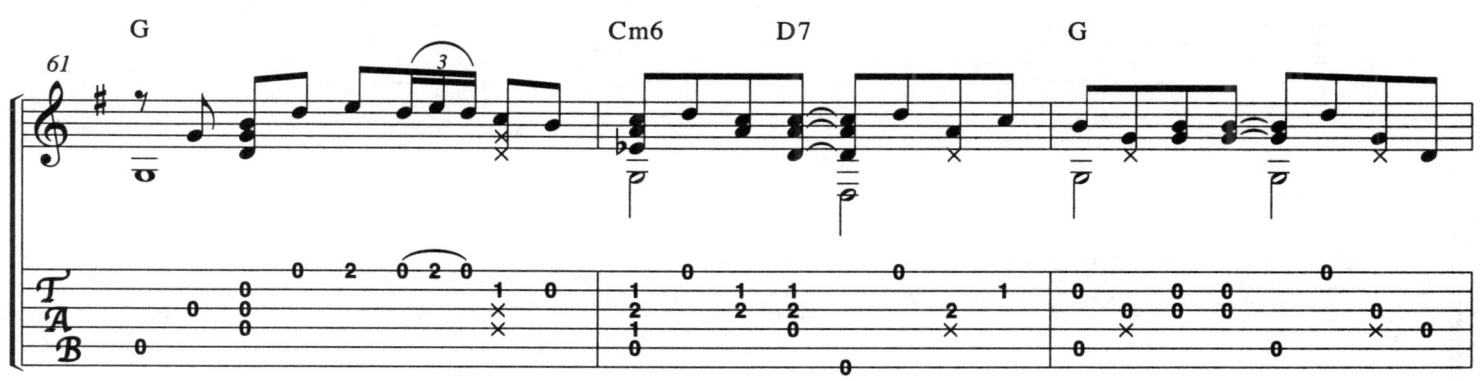
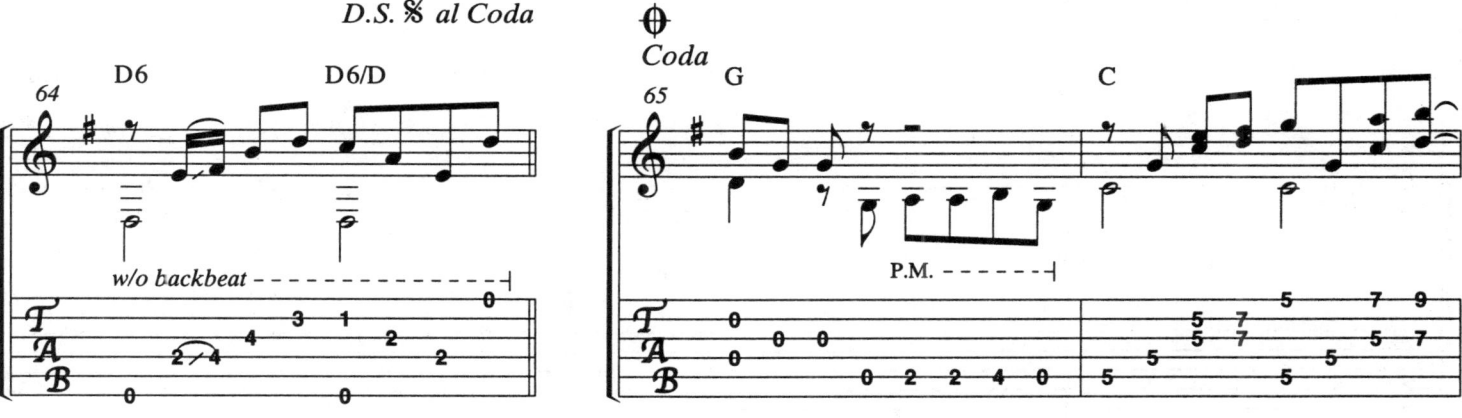
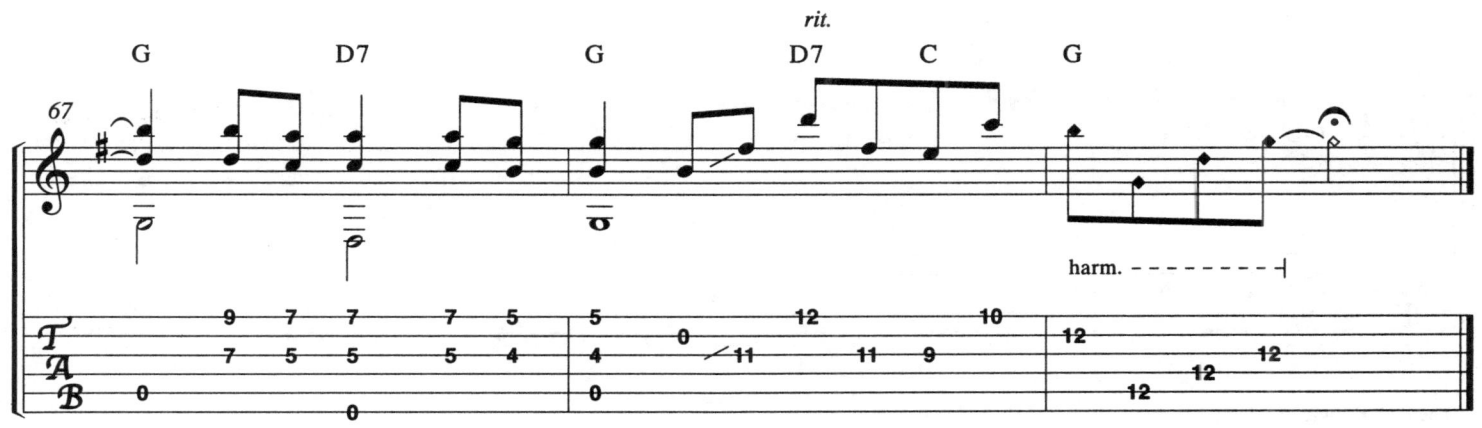

The Sick Boogie

By KENNY SULTAN

Moderately fast swing, in 2 ♩ = 120

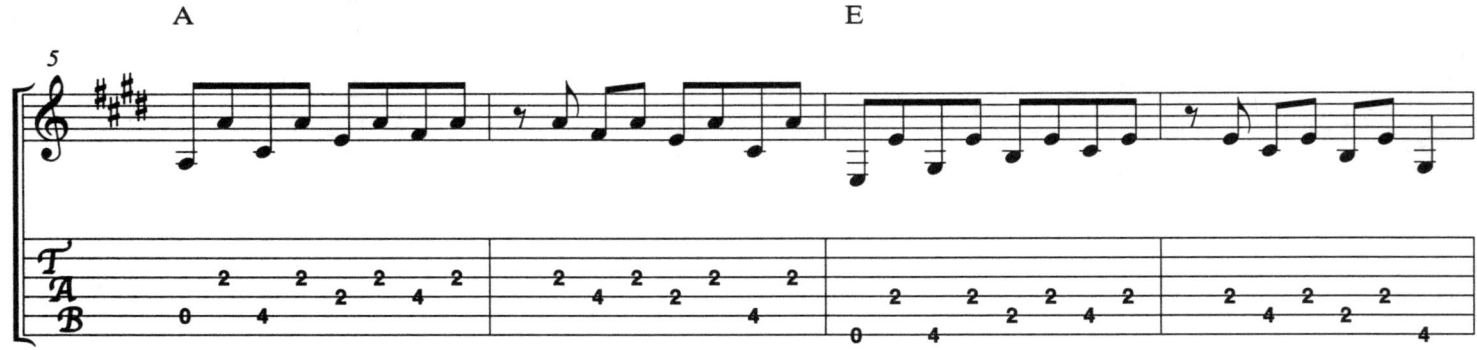
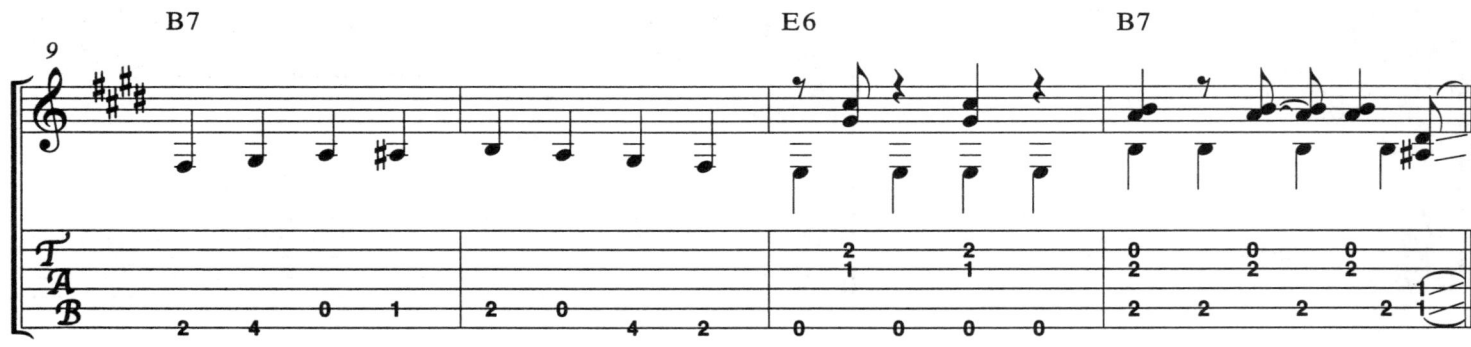
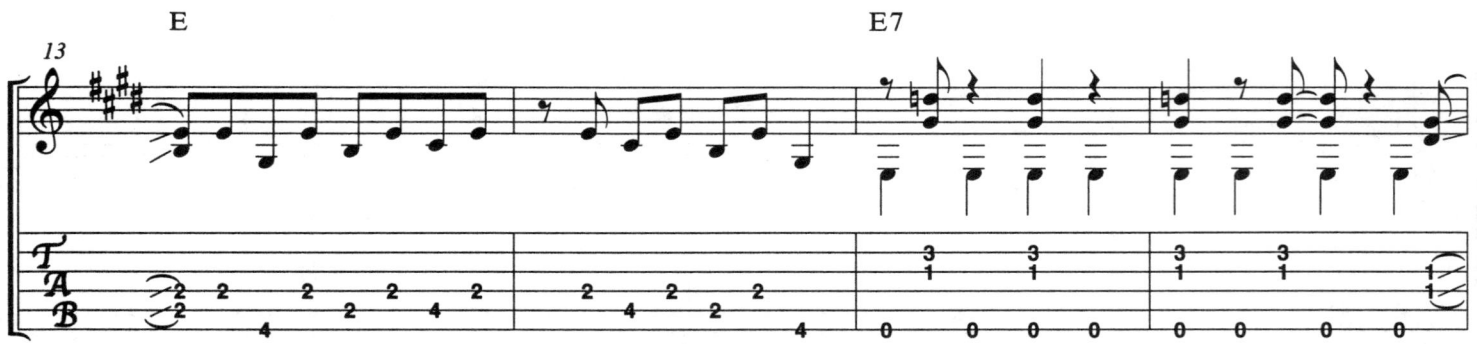

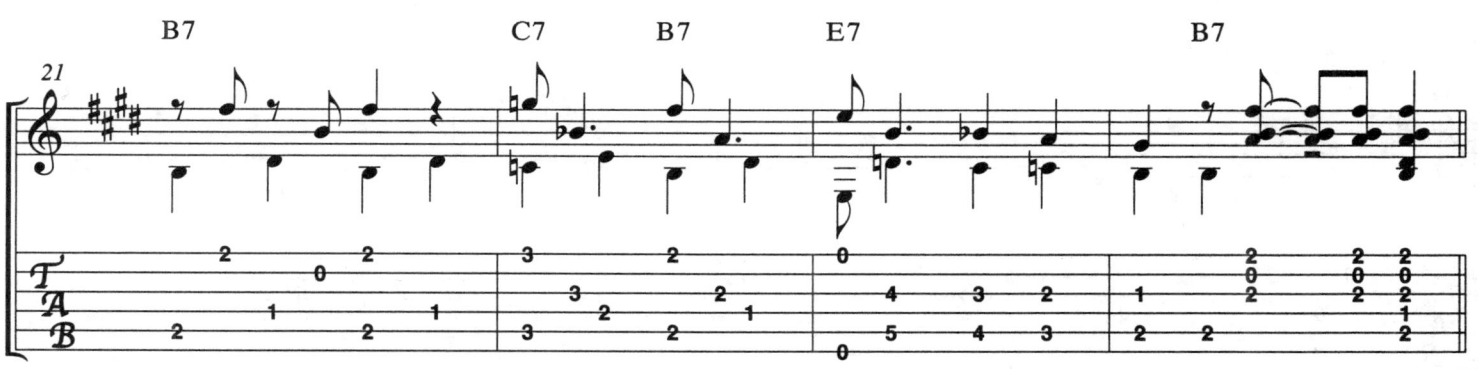
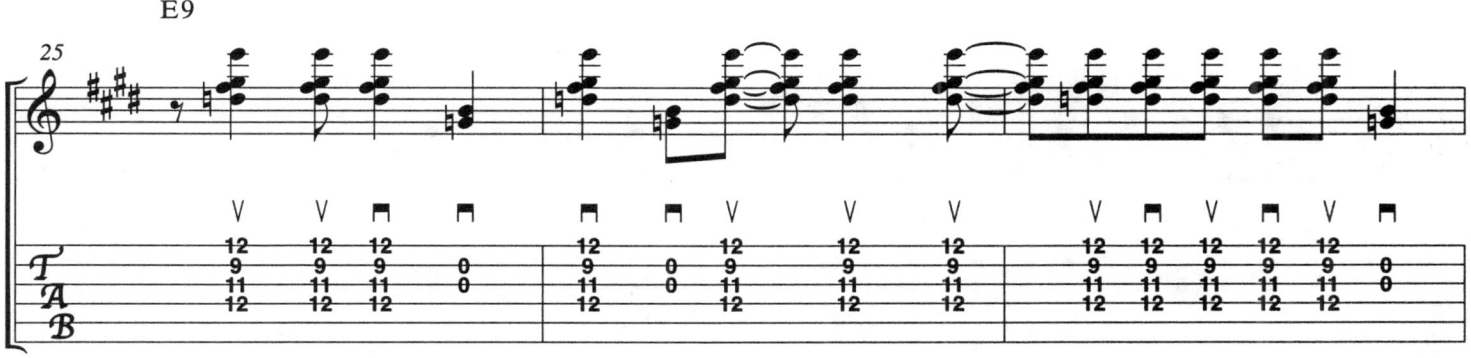
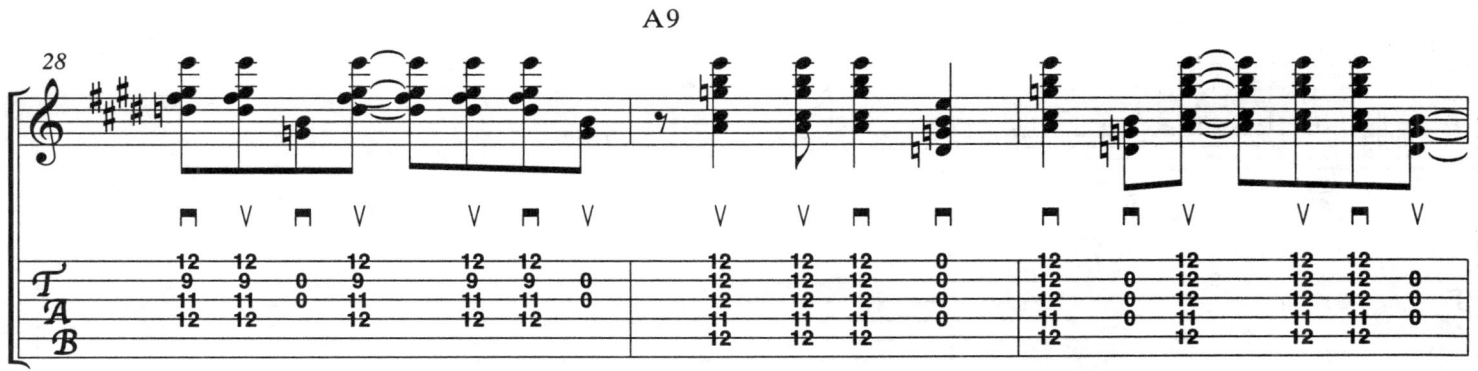

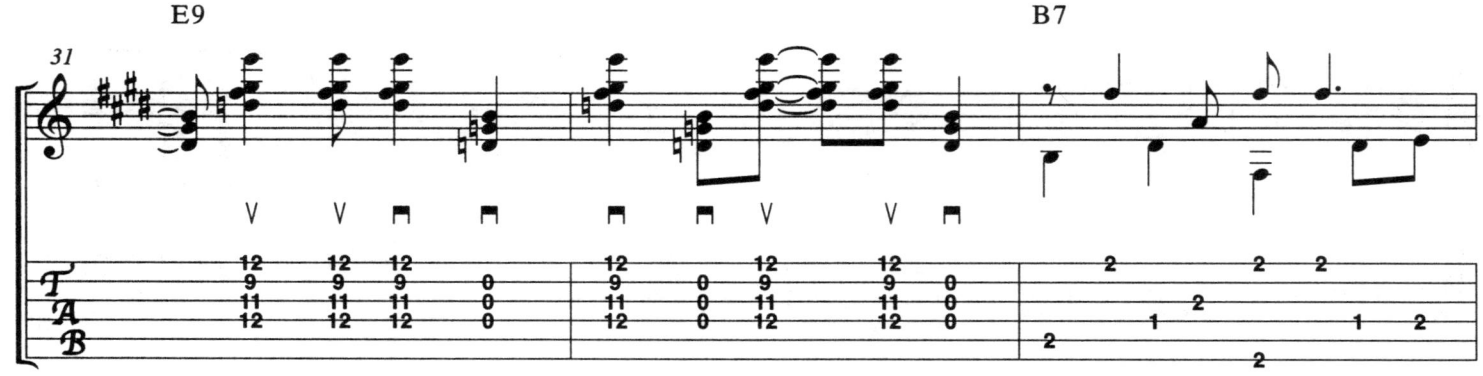
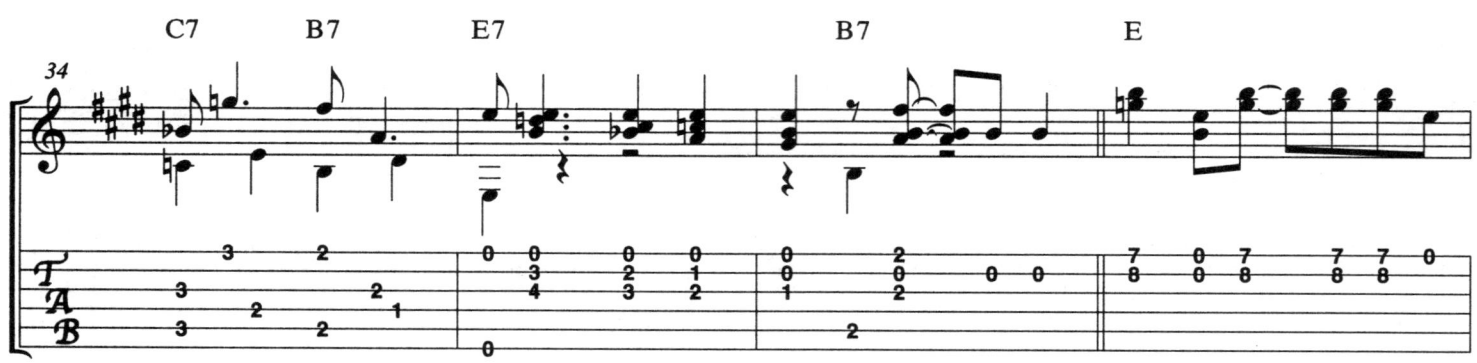

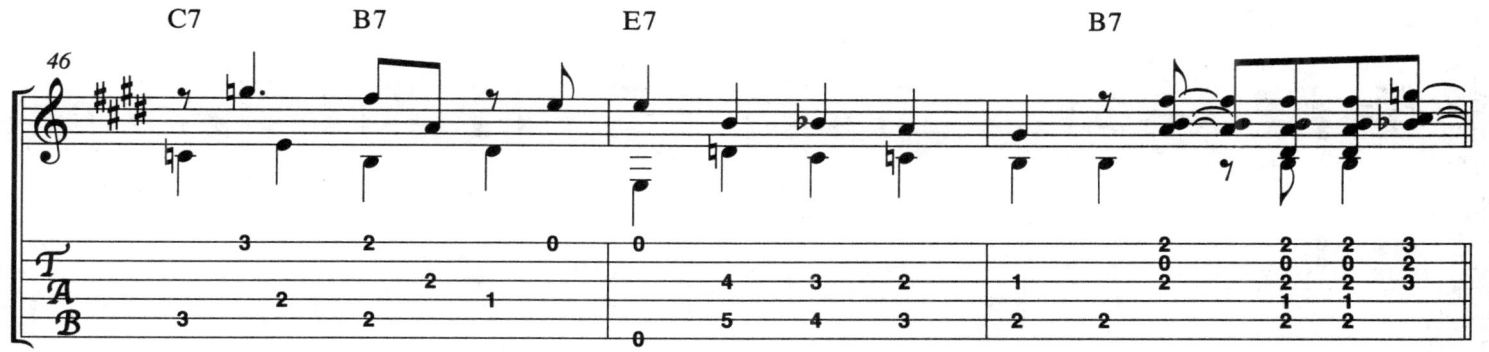

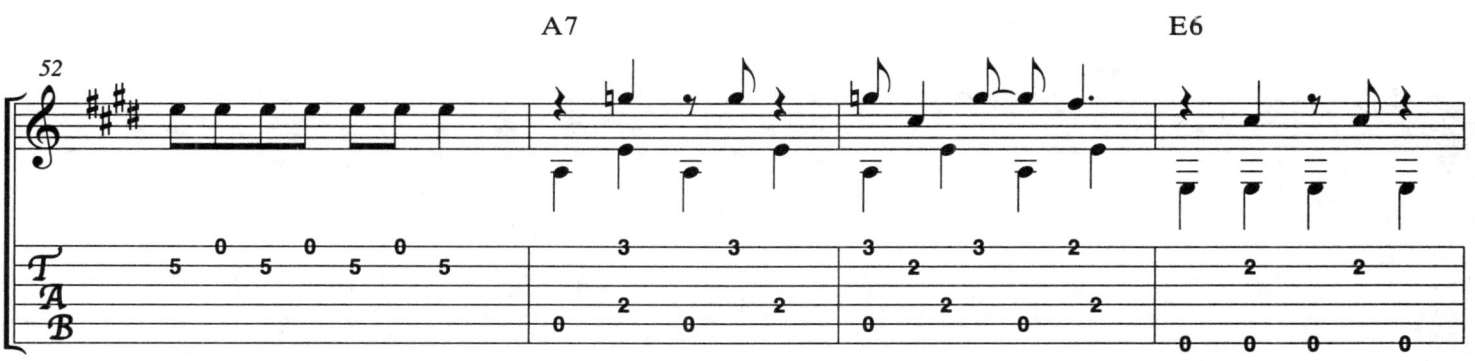
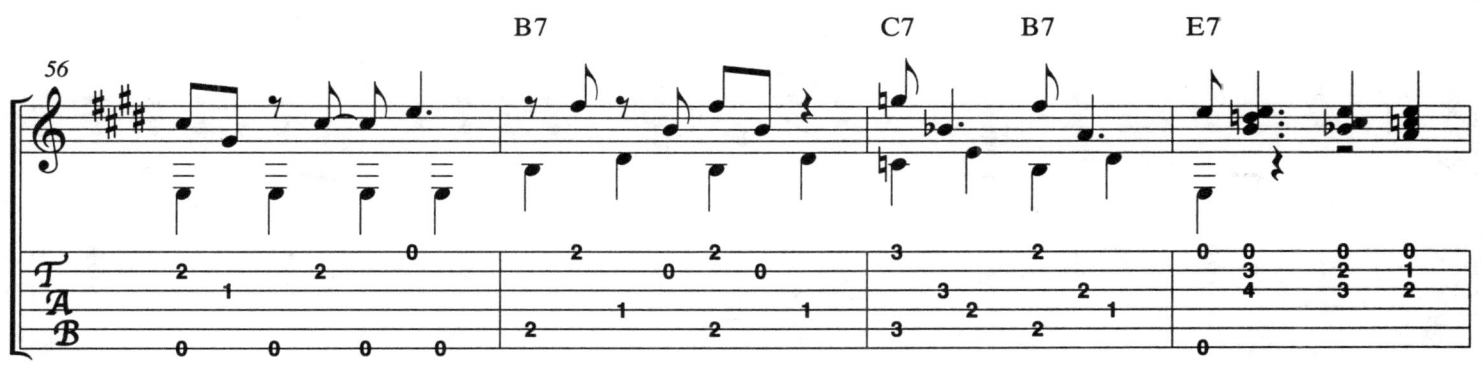

80

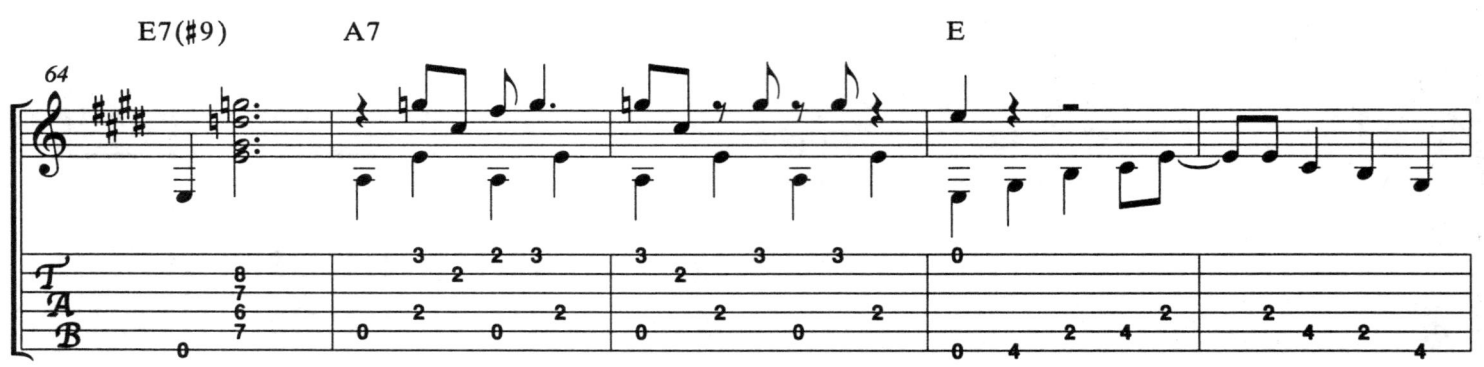
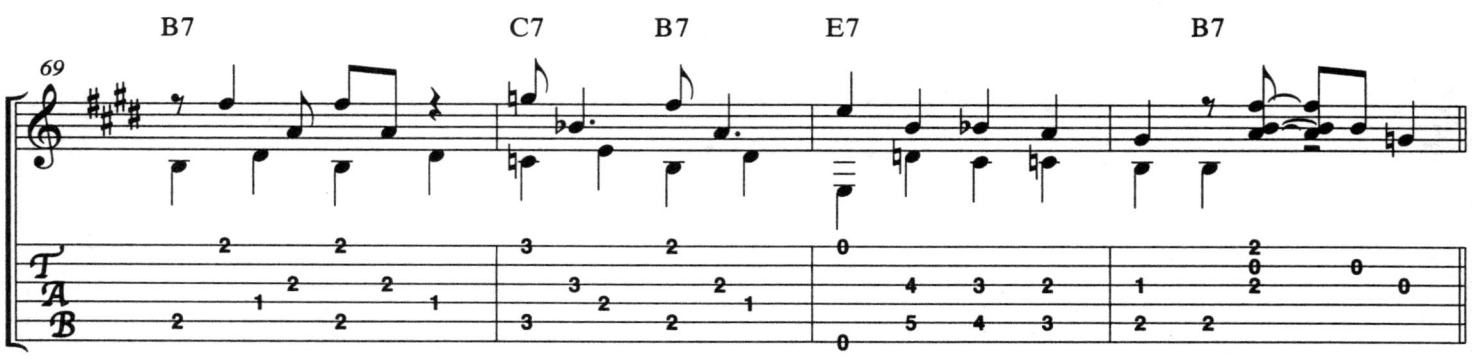

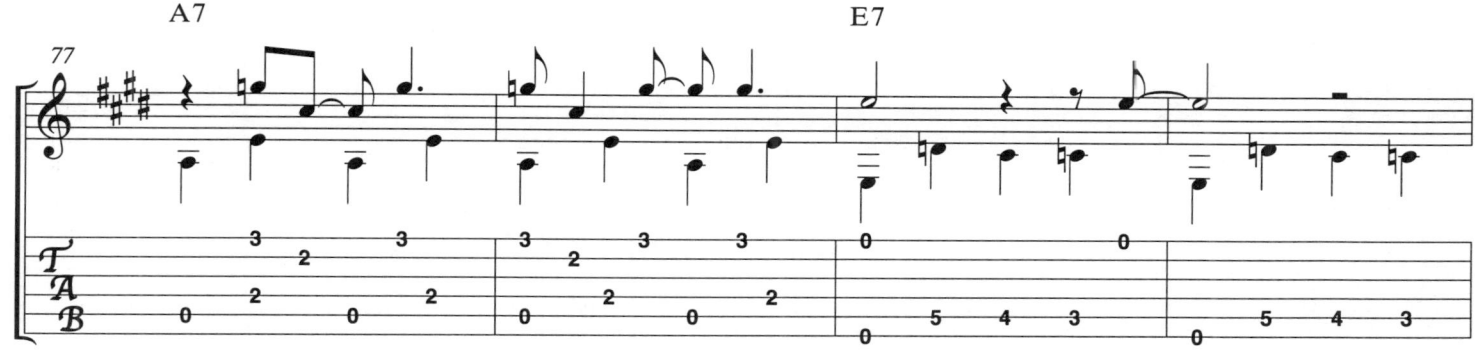
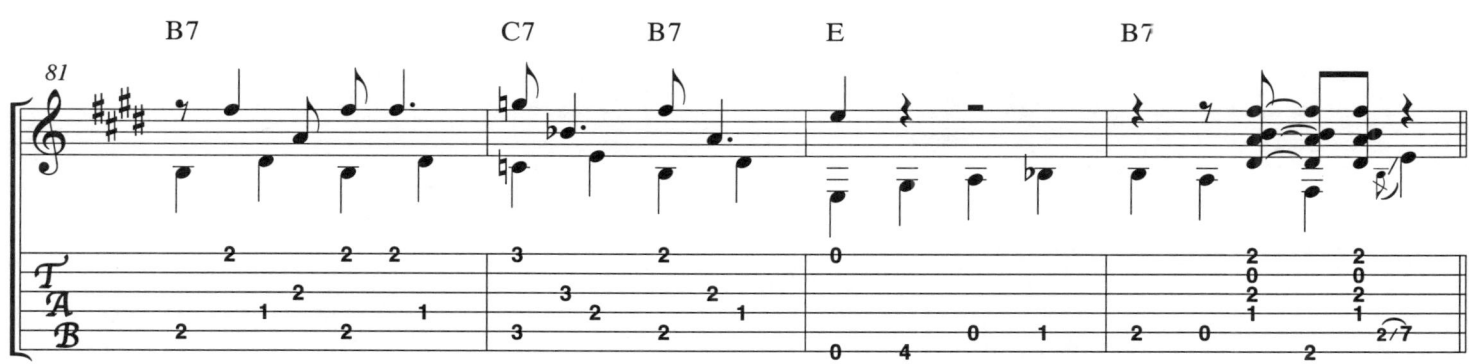
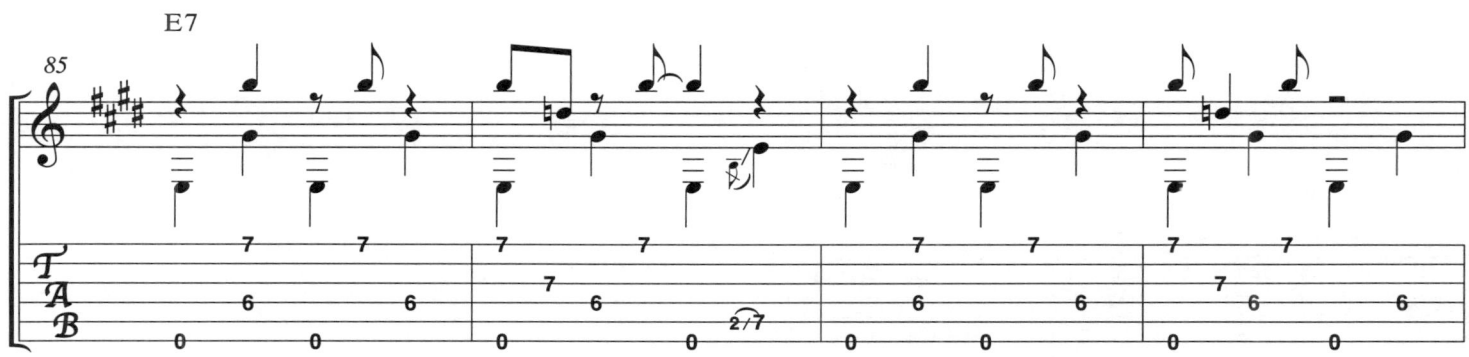
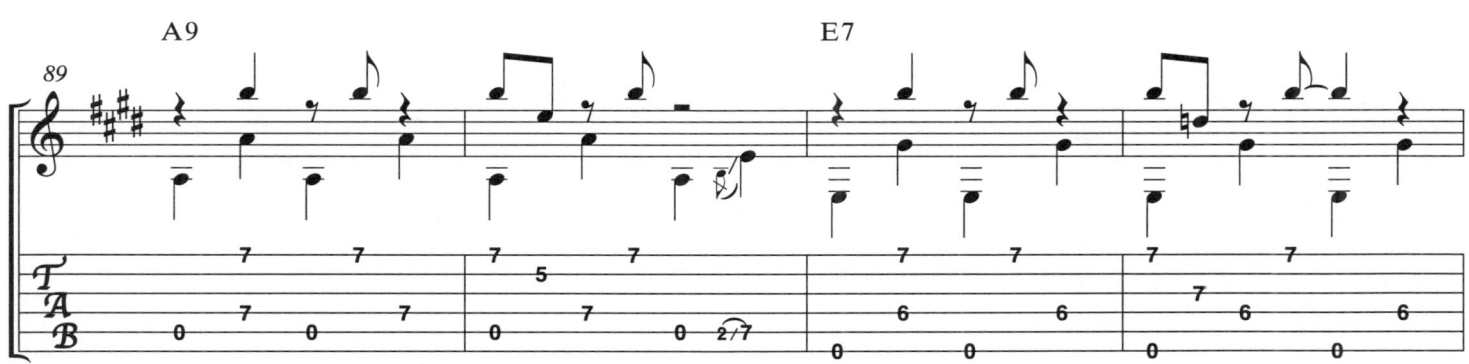

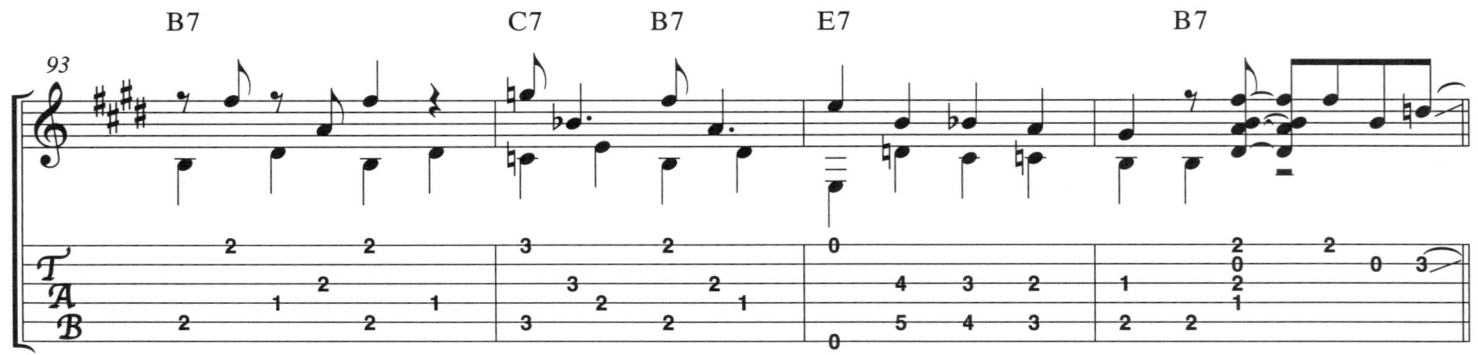
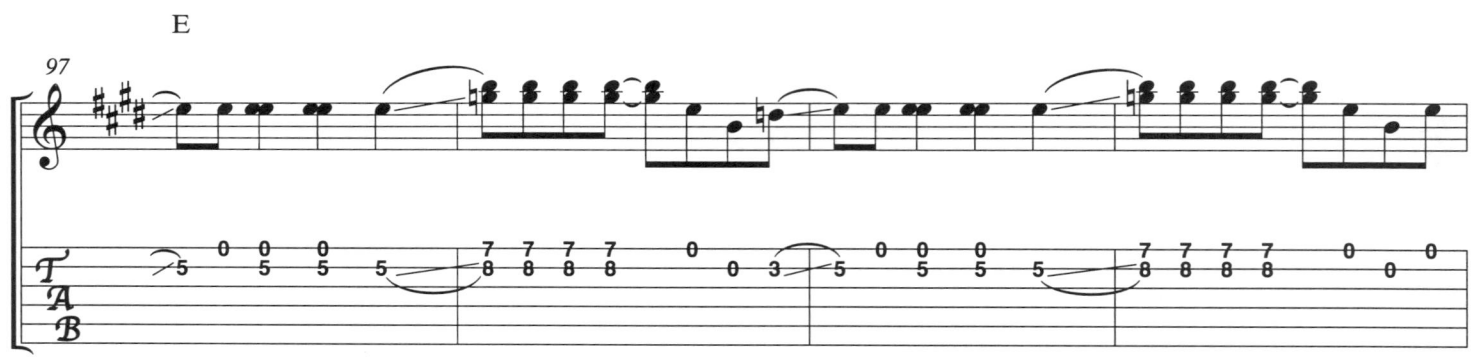
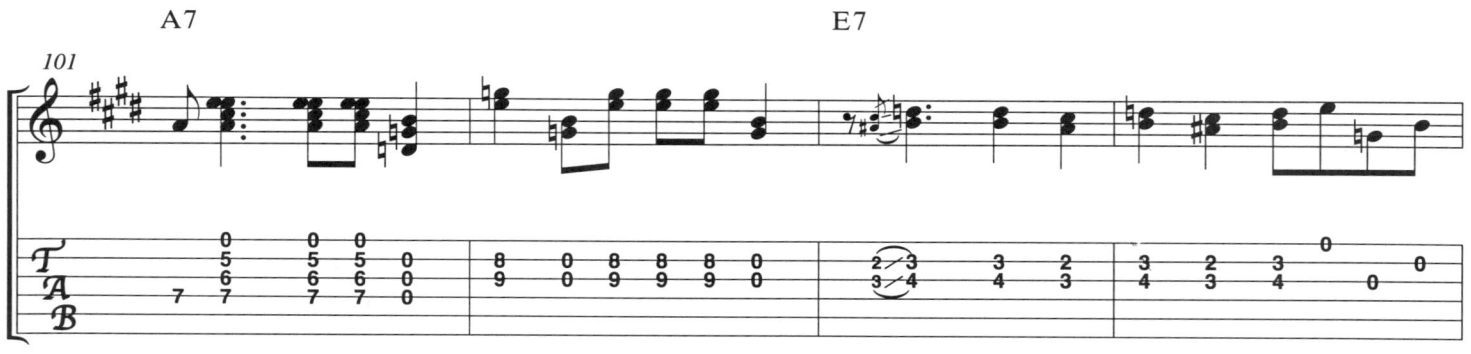
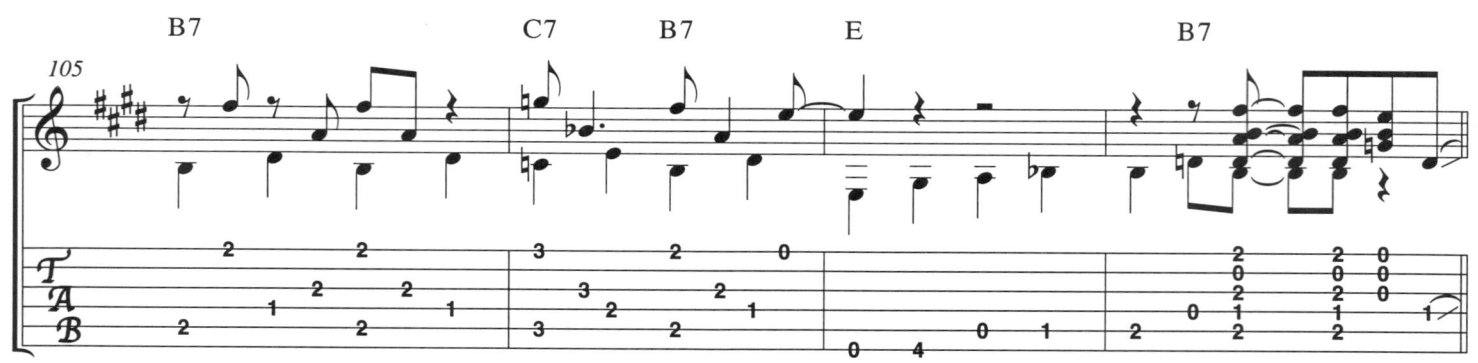

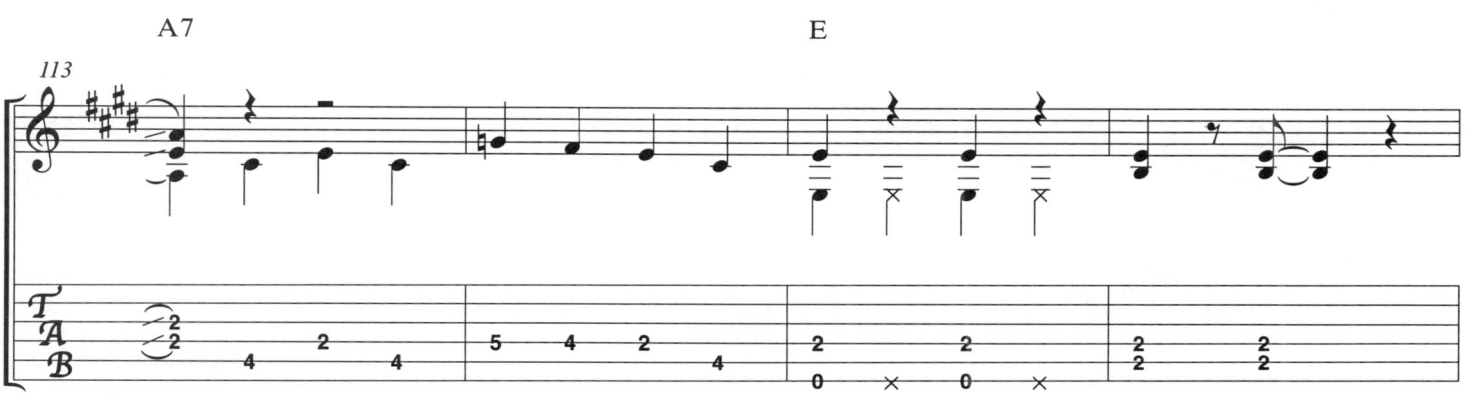
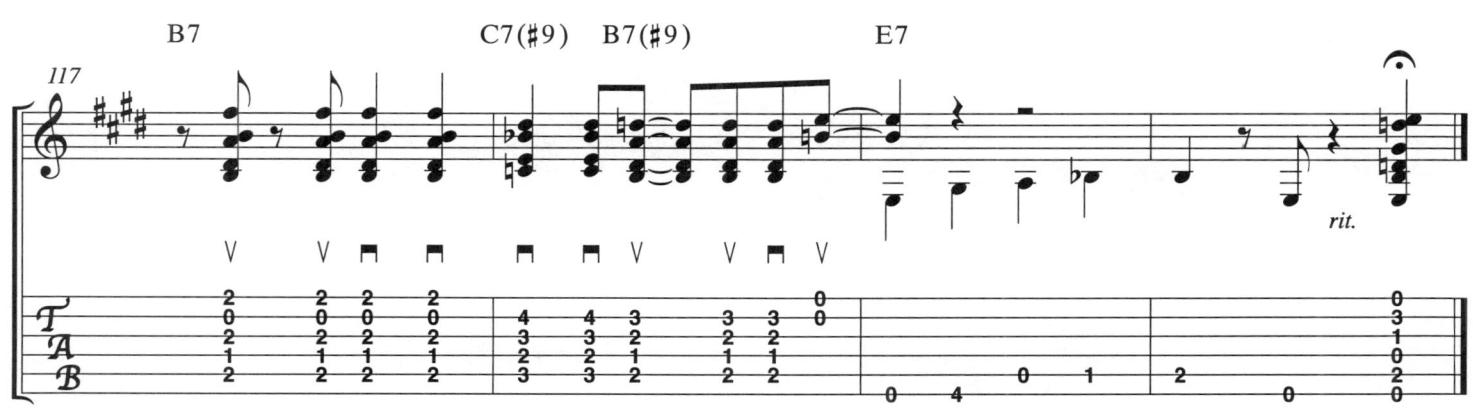

The Sick Boogie - 8 - 8
SAIR011

Acoustic Solo Series

Solo Series

Mike Dowling
Al Petteway
Kenny Sultan

David Cullen
Mike Dowling
Laurence Juber
Al Petteway
Doug Smith
Kenny Sultan

Laurence Juber
Al Petteway
Doug Smith

Acoustic Solo Series DVD Features

- **Play** puts you in Concert Mode, which will play all performances and lessons in sequence.
- **Master Class** lets you pick individual tunes from the menu.
- **Multi-Angle** allows you to select from three different camera angles (available on the lesson segments).
- Complete, printable guitar tab arrangements for every song are embedded on each DVD-ROM in PDF format.